The Practice a of Bolshe

Bertrand Russell

Alpha Editions

This edition published in 2024

ISBN 9789361473784

Design and Setting By

Alpha Editions
www.alphaedis.com

Email - info@alphaedis.com

As per information held with us this book is in Public Domain.
This book is a reproduction of an important historical work.
Alpha Editions uses the best technology to reproduce historical work
in the same manner it was first published to preserve its original nature.
Any marks or number seen are left intentionally to preserve.

Contents

PREFACE — - 1 -
I WHAT IS HOPED FROM BOLSHEVISM — - 4 -
II GENERAL CHARACTERISTICS — - 8 -
III LENIN, TROTSKY AND GORKY — - 14 -
IV ART AND EDUCATION — - 19 -
V COMMUNISM AND THE SOVIET CONSTITUTION — - 32 -
VI THE FAILURE OF RUSSIAN INDUSTRY — - 37 -
VII DAILY LIFE IN MOSCOW — - 43 -
VIII TOWN AND COUNTRY — - 47 -
IX INTERNATIONAL POLICY — - 51 -
PART II BOLSHEVIK THEORY — - 57 -
I THE MATERIALISTIC THEORY OF HISTORY — - 58 -
II DECIDING FORCES IN POLITICS — - 62 -
III BOLSHEVIK CRITICISM OF DEMOCRACY — - 65 -
IV REVOLUTION AND DICTATORSHIP — - 70 -
V MECHANISM AND THE INDIVIDUAL — - 75 -
VI WHY RUSSIAN COMMUNISM HAS FAILED — - 79 -
VII CONDITIONS FOR THE SUCCESS OF COMMUNISM — - 85 -

PREFACEToC

The Russian Revolution is one of the great heroic events of the world's history. It is natural to compare it to the French Revolution, but it is in fact something of even more importance. It does more to change daily life and the structure of society: it also does more to change men's beliefs. The difference is exemplified by the difference between Marx and Rousseau: the latter sentimental and soft, appealing to emotion, obliterating sharp outlines; the former systematic like Hegel, full of hard intellectual content, appealing to historic necessity and the technical development of industry, suggesting a view of human beings as puppets in the grip of omnipotent material forces. Bolshevism combines the characteristics of the French Revolution with those of the rise of Islam; and the result is something radically new, which can only be understood by a patient and passionate effort of imagination.

Before entering upon any detail, I wish to state, as clearly and unambiguously as I can, my own attitude towards this new thing.

By far the most important aspect of the Russian Revolution is as an attempt to realize Communism. I believe that Communism is necessary to the world, and I believe that the heroism of Russia has fired men's hopes in a way which was essential to the realization of Communism in the future. Regarded as a splendid attempt, without which ultimate success would have been very improbable, Bolshevism deserves the gratitude and admiration of all the progressive part of mankind.

But the method by which Moscow aims at establishing Communism is a pioneer method, rough and dangerous, too heroic to count the cost of the opposition it arouses. I do not believe that by this method a stable or desirable form of Communism can be established. Three issues seem to me possible from the present situation. The first is the ultimate defeat of Bolshevism by the forces of capitalism. The second is the victory of the Bolshevists accompanied by a complete loss of their ideals and a régime of Napoleonic imperialism. The third is a prolonged world-war, in which civilization will go under, and all its manifestations (including Communism) will be forgotten.

It is because I do not believe that the methods of the Third International can lead to the desired goal that I have thought it worth while to point out what seem to me undesirable features in the present state of Russia. I think there are lessons to be learnt which must be learnt if the world is ever to achieve what is desired by those in the West who have sympathy with the original aims of the Bolsheviks. I do not think these lessons can be learnt except by facing frankly and fully whatever elements of failure there are in Russia. I think these elements of failure are less attributable to faults of detail than to an impatient philosophy, which aims at creating a new world without sufficient preparation in the opinions and feelings of ordinary men and women.

But although I do not believe that Communism can be realized immediately by the spread of Bolshevism, I do believe that, if Bolshevism falls, it will have contributed a legend and a heroic attempt without which ultimate success might never have come. A fundamental economic reconstruction, bringing with it very far-reaching changes in ways of thinking and feeling, in philosophy and art and private relations, seems absolutely necessary if industrialism is to become the servant of man instead of his master. In all this, I am at one with the Bolsheviks; politically, I criticize them only when their methods seem to involve a departure from their own ideals.

There is, however, another aspect of Bolshevism from which I differ more fundamentally. Bolshevism is not merely a political doctrine; it is also a religion, with elaborate dogmas and inspired scriptures. When Lenin wishes to prove some proposition, he does so, if possible, by quoting texts from Marx and Engels. A full-fledged Communist is not merely a man who believes that land and capital should be held in common, and their produce distributed as nearly equally as possible. He is a man who entertains a number of elaborate and dogmatic beliefs—such as philosophic materialism, for example—which may be true, but are not, to a scientific temper, capable of being known to be true with any certainty. This habit, of militant certainty about objectively doubtful matters, is one from which, since the Renaissance, the world has been gradually emerging, into that temper of constructive and fruitful scepticism which constitutes the scientific outlook. I believe the scientific outlook to be immeasurably important to the human race. If a more just economic system were only attainable by closing men's minds against free inquiry, and plunging them back into the intellectual prison of the middle ages, I should consider the price too high. It cannot be denied that, over any short period of time, dogmatic belief is a help in fighting. If all Communists become religious fanatics, while supporters of capitalism retain a sceptical temper, it may be assumed that the Communists will win, while in the contrary case the capitalists would win. It seems evident, from the attitude of the capitalist world to Soviet Russia, of the Entente to the Central Empires, and of England to Ireland and India, that there is no depth of cruelty, perfidy or brutality from which the present holders of power will shrink when they feel themselves threatened. If, in order to oust them, nothing short of religious fanaticism will serve, it is they who are the prime sources of the resultant evil. And it is permissible to hope that, when they have been dispossessed, fanaticism will fade, as other fanaticisms have faded in the past.

The present holders of power are evil men, and the present manner of life is doomed. To make the transition with a minimum of bloodshed, with a maximum of preservation of whatever has value in our existing civilization, is a difficult problem. It is this problem which has chiefly occupied my mind in writing the following pages. I wish I could think that its solution would be facilitated by some slight degree of moderation and humane feeling on the part of those who enjoy unjust privileges in the world as it is.

The present work is the outcome of a visit to Russia, supplemented by much reading and discussion both before and after. I have thought it best to record what I saw separately from theoretical considerations, and I have endeavoured to state my impressions without any bias for or against the Bolsheviks. I received at their hands the greatest kindness and courtesy, and I owe them a debt of gratitude for the perfect freedom which they allowed me in my investigations. I am conscious that I was too short a time in Russia to be able to form really reliable judgments; however, I share this drawback with most other westerners who have written on Russia since the October Revolution. I feel that Bolshevism is a matter of such importance that it is necessary, for almost every political question, to define one's attitude in regard to it; and I have hopes that I may help others to define their attitude, even if only by way of opposition to what I have written.

I have received invaluable assistance from my secretary, Miss D.W. Black, who was in Russia shortly after I had left. The chapter on Art and Education is written by her throughout. Neither is responsible for the other's opinions.

BERTRAND RUSSELL

September, 1920.

IToC
WHAT IS HOPED FROM BOLSHEVISM

To understand Bolshevism it is not sufficient to know facts; it is necessary also to enter with sympathy or imagination into a new spirit. The chief thing that the Bolsheviks have done is to create a hope, or at any rate to make strong and widespread a hope which was formerly confined to a few. This aspect of the movement is as easy to grasp at a distance as it is in Russia—perhaps even easier, because in Russia present circumstances tend to obscure the view of the distant future. But the actual situation in Russia can only be understood superficially if we forget the hope which is the motive power of the whole. One might as well describe the Thebaid without mentioning that the hermits expected eternal bliss as the reward of their sacrifices here on earth.

I cannot share the hopes of the Bolsheviks any more than those of the Egyptian anchorites; I regard both as tragic delusions, destined to bring upon the world centuries of darkness and futile violence. The principles of the Sermon on the Mount are admirable, but their effect upon average human nature was very different from what was intended. Those who followed Christ did not learn to love their enemies or to turn the other cheek. They learned instead to use the Inquisition and the stake, to subject the human intellect to the yoke of an ignorant and intolerant priesthood, to degrade art and extinguish science for a thousand years. These were the inevitable results, not of the teaching, but of fanatical belief in the teaching. The hopes which inspire Communism are, in the main, as admirable as those instilled by the Sermon on the Mount, but they are held as fanatically, and are likely to do as much harm. Cruelty lurks in our instincts, and fanaticism is a camouflage for cruelty. Fanatics are seldom genuinely humane, and those who sincerely dread cruelty will be slow to adopt a fanatical creed. I do not know whether Bolshevism can be prevented from acquiring universal power. But even if it cannot, I am persuaded that those who stand out against it, not from love of ancient injustice, but in the name of the free spirit of Man, will be the bearers of the seeds of progress, from which, when the world's gestation is accomplished, new life will be born.

The war has left throughout Europe a mood of disillusionment and despair which calls aloud for a new religion, as the only force capable of giving men the energy to live vigorously. Bolshevism has supplied the new religion. It promises glorious things: an end of the injustice of rich and poor, an end of economic slavery, an end of war. It promises an end of the disunion of classes which poisons political life and threatens our industrial system with destruction. It promises an end to commercialism, that subtle falsehood that leads men to appraise everything by its money value, and to determine money value often merely by the caprices of idle plutocrats. It promises a world where all men and women shall be kept sane by work, and where all work shall be of value to the community, not only to a few wealthy vampires. It is to sweep away listlessness and pessimism and weariness and all the complicated miseries of those whose circumstances allow idleness and whose energies are not sufficient to force activity. In place of palaces and hovels, futile vice and useless misery, there is to be wholesome work, enough but not too much, all of it useful, performed by men and women who have no time for pessimism and no occasion for despair.

The existing capitalist system is doomed. Its injustice is so glaring that only ignorance and tradition could lead wage-earners to tolerate it. As ignorance diminishes, tradition becomes weakened, and the war destroyed the hold upon men's minds of everything merely traditional. It may be that, through the influence of America, the capitalist system will linger for another fifty years; but it will grow continually weaker, and can never recover the position of easy dominance which it held in the nineteenth century. To attempt to bolster it up is a useless diversion of energies which might be expended upon building something new. Whether the new thing will be Bolshevism or something else, I do not know; whether it will be better or worse than capitalism, I do not know. But that a radically new order of society will emerge, I feel no doubt. And I also feel no doubt that the new order will be either some form of Socialism or a reversion to barbarism and petty war such as occurred during the barbarian invasion. If Bolshevism remains the only vigorous and effective competitor of capitalism, I believe that no form of Socialism will be realized, but only chaos and destruction. This belief, for which I shall give reasons later, is one of the grounds upon which I oppose Bolshevism. But to oppose it from the point of view of a supporter of capitalism would be, to my mind, utterly futile and against the movement of history in the present age.

The effect of Bolshevism as a revolutionary hope is greater outside Russia than within the Soviet Republic. Grim realities have done much to kill hope among those who are subject to the dictatorship of Moscow. Yet even within Russia, the Communist party, in whose hands all political power is concentrated, still lives by hope, though the pressure of events has made the hope severe and stern and somewhat remote. It is this hope that leads to concentration upon the rising generation. Russian Communists often avow that there is little hope for those who are already adult, and that happiness can only come to the children who have grown up under the new régime and been moulded from the first to the group-mentality that

Communism requires. It is only after the lapse of a generation that they hope to create a Russia that shall realize their vision.

In the Western World, the hope inspired by Bolshevism is more immediate, less shot through with tragedy. Western Socialists who have visited Russia have seen fit to suppress the harsher features of the present régime, and have disseminated a belief among their followers that the millennium would be quickly realized there if there were no war and no blockade. Even those Socialists who are not Bolsheviks for their own country have mostly done very little to help men in appraising the merits or demerits of Bolshevik methods. By this lack of courage they have exposed Western Socialism to the danger of becoming Bolshevik through ignorance of the price that has to be paid and of the uncertainty as to whether the desired goal will be reached in the end. I believe that the West is capable of adopting less painful and more certain methods of reaching Socialism than those that have seemed necessary in Russia. And I believe that while some forms of Socialism are immeasurably better than capitalism, others are even worse. Among those that are worse I reckon the form which is being achieved in Russia, not only in itself, but as a more insuperable barrier to further progress.

In judging of Bolshevism from what is to be seen in Russia at present, it is necessary to disentangle various factors which contribute to a single result. To begin with, Russia is one of the nations that were defeated in the war; this has produced a set of circumstances resembling those found in Germany and Austria. The food problem, for example, appears to be essentially similar in all three countries. In order to arrive at what is specifically Bolshevik, we must first eliminate what is merely characteristic of a country which has suffered military disaster. Next we come to factors which are Russian, which Russian Communists share with other Russians, but not with other Communists. There is, for example, a great deal of disorder and chaos and waste, which shocks Westerners (especially Germans) even when they are in close political sympathy with the Bolsheviks. My own belief is that, although, with the exception of a few very able men, the Russian Government is less efficient in organization than the Germans or the Americans would be in similar circumstances, yet it represents what is most efficient in Russia, and does more to prevent chaos than any possible alternative government would do. Again, the intolerance and lack of liberty which has been inherited from the Tsarist régime is probably to be regarded as Russian rather than Communist. If a Communist Party were to acquire power in England, it would probably be met by a less irresponsible opposition, and would be able to show itself far more tolerant than any government can hope to be in Russia if it is to escape assassination. This, however, is a matter of degree. A great part of the despotism which characterizes the Bolsheviks belongs to the essence of their social philosophy, and would have to be reproduced, even if in a milder form, wherever that philosophy became dominant.

It is customary among the apologists of Bolshevism in the West to excuse its harshness on the ground that it has been produced by the necessity of fighting the Entente and its mercenaries. Undoubtedly it is true that this necessity has produced many of the worst elements in the present state of affairs. Undoubtedly, also, the Entente has incurred a heavy load of guilt by its peevish and futile opposition. But the expectation of such opposition was always part of Bolshevik theory. A general hostility to the first Communist State was both foreseen and provoked by the doctrine of the class war. Those who adopt the Bolshevik standpoint must reckon with the embittered hostility of capitalist States; it is not worth while to adopt Bolshevik methods unless they can lead to good in spite of this hostility. To say that capitalists are wicked and we have no responsibility for their acts is unscientific; it is, in particular, contrary to the Marxian doctrine of economic determinism. The evils produced in Russia by the enmity of the Entente are therefore to be reckoned as essential in the Bolshevik method of transition to Communism, not as specially Russian. I am not sure that we cannot even go a step further. The exhaustion and misery caused by unsuccessful war were necessary to the success of the Bolsheviks; a prosperous population will not embark by such methods upon a fundamental economic reconstruction. One can imagine England becoming Bolshevik after an unsuccessful war involving the loss of India—no improbable contingency in the next few years. But at present the average wage-earner in England will not risk what he has for the doubtful gain of a revolution. A condition of widespread misery may, therefore, be taken as indispensable to the inauguration of Communism, unless, indeed, it were possible to establish Communism more or less peacefully, by methods which would not, even temporarily, destroy the economic life of the country. If the hopes which inspired Communism at the start, and which still inspire its Western advocates, are ever to be realized, the problem of minimizing violence in the transition must be faced. Unfortunately, violence is in itself delightful to most really vigorous revolutionaries, and they feel no interest in the problem of avoiding it as far as possible. Hatred of enemies is easier and more intense than love of friends. But from men who are more anxious to injure opponents than to benefit the world at large no great good is to be expected.

II
GENERAL CHARACTERISTICS

I entered Soviet Russia on May 11th and recrossed the frontier on June 16th. The Russian authorities only admitted me on the express condition that I should travel with the British Labour Delegation, a condition with which I was naturally very willing to comply, and which that Delegation kindly allowed me to fulfil. We were conveyed from the frontier to Petrograd, as well as on subsequent journeys, in a special *train de luxe*; covered with mottoes about the Social Revolution and the Proletariat of all countries; we were received everywhere by regiments of soldiers, with the Internationale being played on the regimental band while civilians stood bare-headed and soldiers at the salute; congratulatory orations were made by local leaders and answered by prominent Communists who accompanied us; the entrances to the carriages were guarded by magnificent Bashkir cavalry-men in resplendent uniforms; in short, everything was done to make us feel like the Prince of Wales. Innumerable functions were arranged for us: banquets, public meetings, military reviews, etc.

The assumption was that we had come to testify to the solidarity of British Labour with Russian Communism, and on that assumption the utmost possible use was made of us for Bolshevik propaganda. We, on the other hand, desired to ascertain what we could of Russian conditions and Russian methods of government, which was impossible in the atmosphere of a royal progress. Hence arose an amicable contest, degenerating at times into a game of hide and seek: while they assured us how splendid the banquet or parade was going to be, we tried to explain how much we should prefer a quiet walk in the streets. I, not being a member of the Delegation, felt less obligation than my companions did to attend at propaganda meetings where one knew the speeches by heart beforehand. In this way, I was able, by the help of neutral interpreters, mostly English or American, to have many conversations with casual people whom I met in the streets or on village greens, and to find out how the whole system appears to the ordinary non-political man and woman. The first five days we spent in Petrograd, the next eleven in Moscow. During this time we were living in daily contact with important men in the Government, so that we learned the official point of view without difficulty. I saw also what I could of the intellectuals in both places. We were all allowed complete freedom to see politicians of opposition parties, and we naturally made full use of this freedom. We saw Mensheviks, Social Revolutionaries of different groups, and Anarchists; we saw them without the presence of any Bolsheviks, and they spoke freely after they had overcome their initial fears.

I had an hour's talk with Lenin, virtually *tête-à-tête*; I met Trotsky, though only in company; I spent a night in the country with Kamenev; and I saw a great deal of other men who, though less known outside Russia, are of considerable importance in the Government.

At the end of our time in Moscow we all felt a desire to see something of the country, and to get in touch with the peasants, since they form about 85 per cent, of the population. The Government showed the greatest kindness in meeting our wishes, and it was decided that we should travel down the Volga from Nijni Novgorod to Saratov, stopping at many places, large and small, and talking freely with the inhabitants. I found this part of the time extraordinarily instructive. I learned to know more than I should have thought possible of the life and outlook of peasants, village schoolmasters, small Jew traders, and all kinds of people. Unfortunately, my friend, Clifford Allen, fell ill, and my time was much taken up with him. This had, however, one good result, namely, that I was able to go on with the boat to Astrakhan, as he was too ill to be moved off it. This not only gave me further knowledge of the country, but made me acquainted with Sverdlov, Acting Minister of Transport, who was travelling on the boat to organize the movement of oil from Baku up the Volga, and who was one of the ablest as well as kindest people whom I met in Russia.

One of the first things that I discovered after passing the Red Flag which marks the frontier of Soviet Russia, amid a desolate region of marsh, pine wood, and barbed wire entanglements, was the profound difference between the theories of actual Bolsheviks and the version of those theories current among advanced Socialists in this country. Friends of Russia here think of the dictatorship of the proletariat as merely a new form of representative government, in which only working men and women have votes, and the constituencies are partly occupational, not geographical. They think that "proletariat" means "proletariat," but "dictatorship" does not quite mean "dictatorship." This is the opposite of the truth. When a Russian Communist speaks of dictatorship, he means the word literally, but when he speaks of the proletariat, he means the word in a Pickwickian sense. He means the "class-conscious" part of the proletariat, *i.e.*, the Communist Party. He includes people by no means proletarian (such as Lenin and Tchicherin) who have the right opinions, and he excludes such wage-earners as have not the right opinions, whom he classifies as lackeys of the *bourgeoisie*. The Communist who sincerely believes the party creed is convinced that private property is the root of all evil; he is so certain of this that he shrinks from no measures, however harsh, which seem necessary for constructing and preserving the Communist State. He spares himself as little as he spares others. He works sixteen hours a day, and foregoes his Saturday half-holiday. He volunteers for any difficult or dangerous work which needs to be done, such as clearing away piles of infected corpses left by Kolchak or Denikin. In spite of his position of power and his control of supplies, he lives an austere life. He is not pursuing personal ends, but aiming at the creation of a new social order. The same motives, however, which make him austere make him also ruthless. Marx has taught that Communism is fatally predestined to come about; this fits in with the Oriental traits in the Russian character, and produces a state of mind not unlike that of the early successors of Mahomet. Opposition is crushed without mercy, and without shrinking from the methods of the Tsarist police, many of whom are still employed at their old work. Since all evils are due to private property, the evils of the Bolshevik régime while it has to fight private property will automatically cease as soon as it has succeeded.

These views are the familiar consequences of fanatical belief. To an English mind they reinforce the conviction upon which English life has been based ever since 1688, that kindliness and tolerance are worth all the creeds in the world—a view which, it is true, we do not apply to other nations or to subject races.

In a very novel society it is natural to seek for historical parallels. The baser side of the present Russian Government is most nearly paralleled by the Directoire in France, but on its better side it is closely analogous to the rule of Cromwell. The sincere Communists (and all the older members of the party have proved their sincerity by years of persecution) are not unlike the Puritan soldiers in their stern politico-moral purpose. Cromwell's dealings with Parliament are not unlike Lenin's with the Constituent Assembly. Both, starting from a combination of democracy and religious faith, were driven to sacrifice democracy to religion enforced by military dictatorship. Both tried to compel their countries to live at a higher level of morality and effort than the population found tolerable. Life in modern Russia, as in Puritan England, is in many ways contrary to instinct. And if the Bolsheviks ultimately fall, it will be for the reason for which the Puritans fell: because there comes a point at which men feel that amusement and ease are worth more than all other goods put together.

Far closer than any actual historical parallel is the parallel of Plato's Republic. The Communist Party corresponds to the guardians; the soldiers have about the same status in both; there is in Russia an attempt to deal with family life more or less as Plato suggested. I suppose it may be assumed that every teacher of Plato throughout the world abhors Bolshevism, and that every Bolshevik regards Plato as an antiquated *bourgeois*. Nevertheless, the parallel is extraordinarily exact between Plato's Republic and the régime which the better Bolsheviks are endeavouring to create.

Bolshevism is internally aristocratic and externally militant. The Communists in many ways resemble the British public-school type: they have all the good and bad traits of an aristocracy which is young and vital. They are courageous, energetic, capable of command, always ready to serve the State; on the other hand, they are dictatorial, lacking in ordinary consideration for the plebs. They are practically the sole possessors of power, and they enjoy innumerable advantages in consequence. Most of them, though far from luxurious, have better food than other people. Only people of some political importance can obtain motor-cars or telephones. Permits for railway journeys, for making purchases at the Soviet stores (where prices are about one-fiftieth of what they are in the market), for going to the theatre, and so on, are, of course, easier to obtain for the friends of those in power than for ordinary mortals. In a thousand ways, the Communists have a life which is happier than that of the rest of the community. Above all, they are less exposed to the unwelcome attentions of the police and the extraordinary commission.

The Communist theory of international affairs is exceedingly simple. The revolution foretold by Marx, which is to abolish capitalism throughout the world, happened to begin in Russia, though Marxian theory would seem to demand that it should begin in America. In countries where the revolution has not yet broken out, the sole duty of a Communist is to hasten its advent. Agreements with capitalist States can only be make-shifts, and can never amount on either side to a sincere peace. No real good can come to any country without a bloody revolution: English Labour men may fancy that a peaceful evolution is possible, but they will find their mistake. Lenin told me that he hopes to see a Labour Government in England, and would wish his supporters to work for it, but solely in order that the futility of Parliamentarism may be conclusively demonstrated to the British working man. Nothing will do any real good except the arming of the proletariat and the disarming of the *bourgeoisie*. Those who preach anything else are social traitors or deluded fools.

For my part, after weighing this theory carefully, and after admitting the whole of its indictment of *bourgeois* capitalism, I find myself definitely and strongly opposed to it. The Third International is an organization which exists to promote the class-war and to hasten the advent of revolution everywhere. My objection is not that capitalism is less bad than the Bolsheviks believe, but that Socialism is less good, not in its best form, but in the only form which is likely to be brought about by war. The evils of war, especially of civil war, are certain and very great; the gains to be achieved by victory are problematical. In the course of a desperate struggle, the heritage of civilization is likely to be lost, while hatred, suspicion, and cruelty become normal in the relations of human beings. In order to succeed in war, a concentration of power is necessary, and from concentration of power the very same evils flow as from the capitalist concentration of wealth. For these reasons chiefly, I cannot support any movement which aims at world revolution. The damage to civilization done by revolution in one country may be repaired by the influence of another in which there has been no revolution; but in a universal cataclysm civilization might go under for a thousand years. But while I cannot advocate world revolution, I cannot escape from the conclusion that the Governments of the leading capitalist countries are doing everything to bring it about. Abuse of our power against Germany, Russia, and India (to say nothing of any other countries) may well bring about our downfall, and produce those very evils which the enemies of Bolshevism most dread.

The true Communist is thoroughly international. Lenin, for example, so far as I could judge, is not more concerned with the interests of Russia than with those of other countries; Russia is, at the moment, the protagonist of the social revolution, and, as such, valuable to the world, but Lenin would sacrifice Russia rather than the revolution, if the alternative should ever arise. This is the orthodox attitude, and is no doubt genuine in many of the leaders. But nationalism is natural and instinctive; through pride in the revolution, it grows again even in the breasts of Communists. Through the Polish war, the Bolsheviks have acquired the support of national feeling, and their position in the country has been immensely strengthened.

The only time I saw Trotsky was at the Opera in Moscow. The British Labour Delegation were occupying what had been the Tsar's box. After speaking with us in the ante-chamber, he stepped to the front of the box and stood with folded arms while the house cheered itself hoarse. Then he spoke a few sentences, short and sharp, with military precision, winding up by calling for "three cheers for our brave fellows at the front," to which the audience responded as a London audience would have responded in the autumn of 1914. Trotsky and the Red Army undoubtedly now have behind them a great body of nationalist sentiment. The reconquest of Asiatic Russia has even revived what is essentially an imperialist way of feeling, though this would be indignantly repudiated by many of those in whom I seemed to detect it. Experience of power is inevitably altering Communist theories, and men who control a vast governmental machine can hardly have quite the same outlook on life as they had when they were hunted fugitives. If the Bolsheviks remain in power, it is much to be feared that their Communism will fade, and that they will increasingly resemble any other Asiatic Government—for example, our own Government in India.

FOOTNOTES:

See the article "On the rôle of the Communist Party in the Proletarian Revolution," in *Theses presented to the Second Congress of the Communist International, Petrograd-Moscow, 18 July, 1920*—a valuable work which I possess only in French.

III
LENIN, TROTSKY AND GORKY

Soon after my arrival in Moscow I had an hour's conversation with Lenin in English, which he speaks fairly well. An interpreter was present, but his services were scarcely required. Lenin's room is very bare; it contains a big desk, some maps on the walls, two book-cases, and one comfortable chair for visitors in addition to two or three hard chairs. It is obvious that he has no love of luxury or even comfort. He is very friendly, and apparently simple, entirely without a trace of *hauteur*. If one met him without knowing who he was, one would not guess that he is possessed of great power or even that he is in any way eminent. I have never met a personage so destitute of self-importance. He looks at his visitors very closely, and screws up one eye, which seems to increase alarmingly the penetrating power of the other. He laughs a great deal; at first his laugh seems merely friendly and jolly, but gradually I came to feel it rather grim. He is dictatorial, calm, incapable of fear, extraordinarily devoid of self-seeking, an embodied theory. The materialist conception of history, one feels, is his life-blood. He resembles a professor in his desire to have the theory understood and in his fury with those who misunderstand or disagree, as also in his love of expounding, I got the impression that he despises a great many people and is an intellectual aristocrat.

The first question I asked him was as to how far he recognized the peculiarity of English economic and political conditions? I was anxious to know whether advocacy of violent revolution is an indispensable condition of joining the Third International, although I did not put this question directly because others were asking it officially. His answer was unsatisfactory to me. He admitted that there is little chance of revolution in England now, and that the working man is not yet disgusted with Parliamentary government. But he hopes that this result may be brought about by a Labour Ministry. He thinks that, if Mr. Henderson, for instance, were to become Prime Minister, nothing of importance would be done; organized Labour would then, so he hopes and believes, turn to revolution. On this ground, he wishes his supporters in this country to do everything in their power to secure a Labour majority in Parliament; he does not advocate abstention from Parliamentary contests, but participation with a view to making Parliament obviously contemptible. The reasons which make attempts at violent revolution seem to most of us both improbable and undesirable in this country carry no weight with him, and seem to him mere *bourgeois* prejudices. When I suggested that whatever is possible in England can be achieved without bloodshed, he waved aside the suggestion as fantastic. I got little impression of knowledge or psychological imagination as regards Great Britain. Indeed the whole tendency of Marxianism is against psychological imagination, since it attributes everything in politics to purely material causes.

I asked him next whether he thought it possible to establish Communism firmly and fully in a country containing such a large majority of peasants. He admitted that it was difficult, and laughed over the exchange the peasant is compelled to make, of food for paper; the worthlessness of Russian paper struck him as comic. But he said—what is no doubt true—that things will right themselves when there are goods to offer to the peasant. For this he looks partly to electrification in industry, which, he says, is a technical necessity in Russia, but will take ten years to complete. He spoke with enthusiasm, as they all do, of the great scheme for generating electrical power by means of peat. Of course he looks to the raising of the blockade as the only radical cure; but he was not very hopeful of this being achieved thoroughly or permanently except through revolutions in other countries. Peace between Bolshevik Russia and capitalist countries, he said, must always be insecure; the Entente might be led by weariness and mutual dissensions to conclude peace, but he felt convinced that the peace would be of brief duration. I found in him, as in almost all leading Communists, much less eagerness than existed in our delegation for peace and the raising of the blockade. He believes that nothing of real value can be achieved except through world revolution and the abolition of capitalism; I felt that he regarded the resumption of trade with capitalist countries as a mere palliative of doubtful value.

He described the division between rich and poor peasants, and the Government propaganda among the latter against the former, leading to acts of violence which he seemed to find amusing. He spoke as though the dictatorship over the peasant would have to continue a long time, because of the peasant's desire for free trade. He said he knew from statistics (what I can well believe) that the peasants have had more to eat these last two years than they ever had before, "and yet they are against us," he added a little wistfully. I asked him what to reply to critics who say that in the country he has merely created peasant proprietorship, not Communism; he replied that that is not quite the truth, but he did not say what the truth is.

The last question I asked him was whether resumption of trade with capitalist countries, if it took place, would not create centres of capitalist influence, and make the preservation of Communism more difficult? It had seemed to me that the more ardent Communists might well dread commercial intercourse with the outer world, as leading to an infiltration of heresy, and making the rigidity of the present system almost impossible. I wished to know whether he had such a feeling. He admitted that trade would create difficulties, but said they would be less than those of the war. He said that two years ago neither he nor his colleagues thought they could survive against the hostility of the world. He attributes their survival to the jealousies and divergent interests of the different capitalist nations; also to the power of Bolshevik propaganda. He said the Germans had laughed when the Bolsheviks proposed to combat guns with leaflets, but that the event had proved the leaflets quite as powerful. I do not think he recognizes that the Labour and Socialist parties have had any part in the matter. He does not seem to know that the attitude of British Labour has done a great deal to make a first-class war against Russia impossible, since it has confined the Government to what could be done in a hole-and-corner way, and denied without a too blatant mendacity.

He thoroughly enjoys the attacks of Lord Northcliffe, to whom he wishes to send a medal for Bolshevik propaganda. Accusations of spoliation, he remarked, may shock the *bourgeois*, but have an opposite effect upon the proletarian.

I think if I had met him without knowing who he was, I should not have guessed that he was a great man; he struck me as too opinionated and narrowly orthodox. His strength comes, I imagine, from his honesty, courage, and unwavering faith—religious faith in the Marxian gospel, which takes the place of the Christian martyr's hopes of Paradise, except that it is less egotistical. He has as little love of liberty as the Christians who suffered under Diocletian, and retaliated when they acquired power. Perhaps love of liberty is incompatible with whole-hearted belief in a panacea for all human ills. If so, I cannot but rejoice in the sceptical temper of the Western world. I went to Russia a Communist; but contact with those who have no doubts has intensified a thousandfold my own doubts, not as to Communism in itself, but as to the wisdom of holding a creed so firmly that for its sake men are willing to inflict widespread misery.

Trotsky, whom the Communists do not by any means regard as Lenin's equal, made more impression upon me from the point of view of intelligence and personality, though not of character. I saw too little of him, however, to have more than a very superficial impression. He has bright eyes, military bearing, lightning intelligence and magnetic personality. He is very good-looking, with admirable wavy hair; one feels he would be irresistible to women. I felt in him a vein of gay good humour, so long as he was not crossed in any way. I thought, perhaps wrongly, that his vanity was even greater than his love of power—the sort of vanity that one associates with an artist or actor. The comparison with Napoleon was forced upon one. But I had no means of estimating the strength of his Communist conviction, which may be very sincere and profound.

An extraordinary contrast to both these men was Gorky, with whom I had a brief interview in Petrograd. He was in bed, apparently very ill and obviously heart-broken. He begged me, in anything I might say about Russia, always to emphasize what Russia has suffered. He supports the Government—as I should do, if I were a Russian—not because he thinks it faultless, but because the possible alternatives are worse. One felt in him a love of the Russian people which makes their present martyrdom almost unbearable, and prevents the fanatical faith by which the pure Marxians are upheld. I felt him the most lovable, and to me the most sympathetic, of all the Russians I saw. I wished for more knowledge of his outlook, but he spoke with difficulty and was constantly interrupted by terrible fits of coughing, so that I could not stay. All the intellectuals whom I met—a class who have suffered terribly—expressed their gratitude to him for what he has done on their behalf. The materialistic conception of history is all very well, but some care for the higher things of civilization is a relief. The Bolsheviks are sometimes said to have done great things for art, but I could not discover that they had done more than preserve something of what existed before. When I questioned one of them on the subject, he grew impatient, and said: "We haven't time for a new art, any more than for a new religion." Unavoidably, although the Government favours art as much as it can, the atmosphere is one in which art cannot flourish, because art is anarchic and resistant to organization. Gorky has done all that one man could to preserve the intellectual and artistic life of Russia. I feared that he was dying, and that, perhaps, it was dying too. But he recovered, and I hope it will recover also.

FOOTNOTES:

Electrification is desired not merely for reorganizing industry, but in order to industrialize agriculture. In *Theses presented to the Second Congress of the Communist International* (an instructive little book, which I shall quote as *Theses*), it is said in an article on the Agrarian question that Socialism will not be secure till industry is reorganized on a new basis with "general application of electric energy in all branches of agriculture and rural economy," which "alone can give to the towns the possibility of offering to backward rural districts a technical and social aid capable of determining an extraordinary increase of productivity of agricultural and rural labour, and of engaging the small cultivators, in their own interest, to pass progressively to a collectivist mechanical cultivation" (p. 36 of French edition).

- In *Theses* (p. 34) it is said: "It would be an irreparable error ... not to admit the gratuitous grant of part of the expropriated lands to poor and even well-to-do peasants."

IV
ART AND EDUCATION

It has often been said that, whatever the inadequacy of Bolshevik organization in other fields, in art and in education at least they have made great progress.

To take first of all art: it is true that they began by recognizing, as perhaps no other revolutionary government would, the importance and spontaneity of the artistic impulse, and therefore while they controlled or destroyed the counter-revolutionary in all other social activities, they allowed the artist, whatever his political creed, complete freedom to continue his work. Moreover, as regards clothing and rations they treated him especially well. This, and the care devoted to the upkeep of churches, public monuments, and museums, are well-known facts, to which there has already been ample testimony.

The preservation of the old artistic community practically intact was the more remarkable in view of the pronounced sympathy of most of them with the old régime. The theory, however, was that art and politics belonged to two separate realms; but great honour would of course be the portion of those artists who would be inspired by the revolution.

Three years' experience, however, have proved the falsity of this doctrine and led to a divorce between art and popular feeling which a sensitive observer cannot fail to remark. It is glaringly apparent in the hitherto most vital of all Russian arts, the theatre. The artists have continued to perform the old classics in tragedy or comedy, and the old-style operette. The theatre programmes have remained the same for the last two years, and, but for the higher standard of artistic performance, might belong to the theatres of Paris or London. As one sits in the theatre, one is so acutely conscious of the discrepancy between the daily life of the audience and that depicted in the play that the latter seems utterly dead and meaningless. To some of the more fiery Communists it appears that a mistake has been made. They complain that *bourgeois* art is being preserved long after its time, they accuse the artists of showing contempt for their public, of being as untouched by the revolutionary mood as an elderly *bourgeoise* bewailing the loss of her personal comfort; they would like to see only the revolutionary mood embodied in art, and to achieve this would make a clean sweep, enforcing the writing and performance of nothing but revolutionary plays and the painting of revolutionary pictures. Nor can it be argued that they are wrong as to the facts: it is plain that the preservation of the old artistic tradition has served very little purpose; but on the other hand it is equally plain that an artist cannot be drilled like a military recruit. There is, fortunately, no sign that these tactics will be directly adopted, but in an indirect fashion they are already being applied. An artist is not to blame if his temperament leads him to draw cartoons of leading Bolsheviks, or satirize the various comical aspects—and they are many—of the Soviet régime. To force such a man, however, to turn his talent only against Denikin, Yudenitch and Kolchak, or the leaders of the Entente, is momentarily good for Communism, but it is discouraging to the artist, and may prove in the long run bad for art, and possibly for Communism also. It is plain from the religious nature of Communism in Russia, that such controlling of the impulse to artistic creation is inevitable, and that propaganda art alone can flourish in such an atmosphere. For example, no poetry or literature that is not orthodox will reach the printing press. It is so easy to make the excuse of lack of paper and the urgent need for manifestoes. Thus there may well come to be a repetition of the attitude of the mediæval Church to the sagas and legends of the people, except that, in this case, it is the folk tales which will be preserved, and the more sensitive and civilized products banned. The only poet who seems to be much spoken of at present in Russia is one who writes rough popular songs. There are revolutionary odes, but one may hazard a guess that they resemble our patriotic war poetry.

I said that this state of affairs may in the long run be bad for art, but the contrary may equally well prove to be the truth. It is of course discouraging and paralysing to the old-style artist, and it is death to the old individual art which depended on subtlety and oddity of temperament, and arose very largely from the complicated psychology of the idle. There it stands, this old art, the purest monument to the nullity of the art-for-art's-sake doctrine, like a rich exotic plant of exquisite beauty, still apparently in its glory, till one perceives that the roots are cut, and that leaf by leaf it is gradually fading away.

But, unlike the Puritans in this respect, the Bolsheviks have not sought to dig up the roots, and there are signs that the paralysis is merely temporary. Moreover, individual art is not the only form, and in particular the plastic arts have shown that they can live by mass action, and flourish under an intolerant faith. Communist artists of the future may erect public buildings surpassing in beauty the mediæval churches, they may paint frescoes, organize pageants, make Homeric songs about their heroes. Communist art will begin, and is beginning now, in the propaganda pictures, and stories such as those designed for peasants and children. There is, for instance, a kind of Rake's Progress or "How she became a Communist," in which the Entente leaders make a sorry and grotesque appearance. Lenin and Trotsky already figure in woodcuts as Moses and

Aaron, deliverers of their people, while the mother and child who illustrate the statistics of the maternity exhibition have the grace and beauty of mediæval madonnas. Russia is only now emerging from the middle ages, and the Church tradition in painting is passing with incredible smoothness into the service of Communist doctrine. These pictures have, too, an oriental flavour: there are brown Madonnas in the Russian churches, and such an one illustrates the statistics of infant mortality in India, while the Russian mother, broad-footed, in gay petticoat and kerchief, sits in a starry meadow suckling her baby from a very ample white breast. I think that this movement towards the Church tradition may be unconscious and instinctive, and would perhaps be deplored by many Communists, for whom grandiose bad Rodin statuary and the crudity of cubism better express what they mean by revolution. But this revolution is Russian and not French, and its art, if all goes well, should inevitably bear the popular Russian stamp. It is would-be primitive and popular art that is vulgar. Such at least is the reflection engendered by an inspection of Russian peasant work as compared with the spirit of *Children's Tales*.

The Russian peasant's artistic impulse is no legend. Besides the carving and embroidery which speak eloquently to peasant skill, one observes many instances in daily life. He will climb down, when his slowly-moving train stops by the wayside, to gather branches and flowers with which he will decorate the railway carriage both inside and out, he will work willingly at any task which has beauty for its object, and was all too prone under the old régime to waste his time and his employer's material in fashioning small metal or wooden objects with his hands.

If the *bourgeois* tradition then will not serve, there is a popular tradition which is still live and passionate and which may perhaps persist. Unhappily it has a formidable enemy in the organization and development of industry, which is far more dangerous to art than Communist doctrine. Indeed, industry in its early stages seems everywhere doomed to be the enemy of beauty and instinctive life. One might hope that this would not prove to be so in Russia, the first Socialist State, as yet unindustrial, able to draw on the industrial experience of the whole world, were it not that one discovers with a certain misgiving in the Bolshevik leaders the rasping arid temperament of those to whom the industrial machine is an end in itself, and, in addition, reflects that these industrially minded men have as yet no practical experience, nor do there exist men of goodwill to help them. It does not seem reasonable to hope that Russia can pass through the period of industrialization without a good deal of mismanagement, involving waste resulting in too long hours, child labour and other evils with which the West is all too familiar. What the Bolsheviks would not therefore willingly do to art, the Juggernaut which they are bent on setting in motion may accomplish for them.

The next generation in Russia will have to consist of practical hard-working men, the old-style artists will die off and successors will not readily arise. A State which is struggling with economic difficulties is bound to be slow to admit an artistic vocation, since this involves exemption from practical work. Moreover the majority of minds always turn instinctively to the real need of the moment. A man therefore who is adapted by talent and temperament to becoming an opera singer, will under the pressure of Communist enthusiasm and Government encouragement turn his attention to economics. (I am here quoting an actual instance.) The whole Russian people at this stage in their development strike one as being forced by the logic of their situation to make a similar choice.

It may be all to the good that there should be fewer professional artists, since some of the finest work has been done by men and groups of men to whom artistic expression was only a pastime. They were not hampered by the solemnity and reverence for art which too often destroy the spontaneity of the professional. Indeed a revival of this attitude to art is one of the good results which may be hoped for from a Communist revolution in a more advanced industrial community. There the problem of education will be to stimulate the creative impulses towards art and science so that men may know how to employ their leisure hours. Work in the factory can never be made to provide an adequate outlet. The only hope, if men are to remain human beings under industrialism, is to reduce hours to the minimum. But this is only possible when production and organization are highly efficient, which will not be the case for a long time in Russia. Hence not only does it appear that the number of artists will grow less, but that the number of people undamaged in their artistic impulses and on that account able to create or appreciate as amateurs is likely to be deplorably small. It is in this damaging effect of industry on human instinct that the immediate danger to art in Russia lies.

The effect of industry on the crafts is quite obvious. A craftsman who is accustomed to work with his hands, following the tradition developed by his ancestors, is useless when brought face to face with a machine. And the man who can handle the machine will only be concerned with quantity and utility in the first instance. Only gradually do the claims of beauty come to be recognized. Compare the modern motor car with the first of its species, or even, since the same law seems to operate in nature, the prehistoric animal with its modern descendant. The same relation exists between them as between man and the ape, or the horse and the hipparion. The movement of life seems to be towards ever greater delicacy and complexity, and man carries it forward in the articles that he makes and the society that he develops. Industry is a new tool, difficult to handle, but it will produce just as beautiful objects as did the mediæval builder and craftsman, though not until it has been in being for a long time and belongs to tradition.

One may expect, therefore, that while the crafts in Russia will lose in artistic value, the drama, sculpture and painting and all those arts which have nothing to do with the machine and depend entirely upon mental and spiritual inspiration will receive an impetus from the Communist faith. Whether the flowering period will be long or short depends partly on the political situation, but chiefly on the rapidity of industrial development. It may be that the machine will ultimately conquer the Communist faith and grind out the human impulses, and Russia become during this transition period as inartistic and soulless as was America until quite recent years. One would like to hope that mechanical progress will be swift and social idealism sufficiently strong to retain control. But the practical difficulties are almost insuperable.

Such signs of the progress of art as it is possible to notice at this early stage would seem to bear out the above argument. For instance, an attempt is being made to foster the continuation of peasant embroidery, carving, &c., in the towns. It is done by people who have evidently lost the tradition already. They are taught to copy the models which are placed in the Peasant Museum, but there is no comparison between the live little wooden lady who smiles beneath the glass case, and the soulless staring-eyed creature who is offered for sale, nor between the quite ordinary carved fowl one may buy and the amusing life-like figure one may merely gaze at.

But when one comes to art directly inspired by Communism it is a different story. Apart from the propaganda pictures already referred to, there are propaganda plays performed by the Red Army in its spare moments, and there are the mass pageant plays performed on State occasions. I had the good fortune to witness one of each kind.

The play was called *Zarevo* (The Dawn), and was performed on a Saturday night on a small stage in a small hall in an entirely amateur fashion. It represented Russian life just before the revolution. It was intense and tragic and passionately acted. Dramatic talent is not rare in Russia. Almost the only comic relief was provided by the Tsarist police, who made one appearance towards the end, got up like comic military characters in a musical comedy—just as, in mediæval miracle plays, the comic character was Satan. The play's intention was to show a typical Russian working-class family. There were the old father, constantly drunk on vodka, alternately maudlin and scolding; the old mother; two sons, the one a Communist and the other an Anarchist; the wife of the Communist, who did dressmaking; her sister, a prostitute; and a young girl of *bourgeois* family, also a

Communist, involved in a plot with the Communist son, who was of course the hero of the play.

The first act revealed the stern and heroic Communist maintaining his views despite the reproaches of father and mother and the nagging of his wife. It showed also the Anarchist brother (as might be expected from the Bolshevik hostility to Anarchism) as an unruly, lazy, ne'er-do-well, with a passionate love for Sonia, the young *bourgeoise*, which was likely to become dangerous if not returned. She, on the other hand, obviously preferred the Communist. It was clear that he returned her love, but it was not quite clear that he would wish the relation to be anything more than platonic comradeship in the service of their common ideal. An unsuccessful strike, bringing want and danger from the police, together with increasing jealousy on the part of the Anarchist, led up to the tragic dénouement. I was not quite definite as to how this was brought about. All violent action was performed off the stage, and this made the plot at times difficult to follow. But it seemed that the Anarchist in a jealous rage forged a letter from his brother to bring Sonia to a rendezvous, and there murdered her, at the same time betraying his brother to the police. When the latter came to effect his arrest, and accuse him also, as the most likely person, of the murder, the Anarchist was seized with remorse and confessed. Both were therefore led away together. Once the plot is sketched, the play calls for no comment. It had not great merit, though it is unwise to hazard a judgment on a play whose dialogue was not fully interpreted, but it was certainly real, and the link between audience and performers was established as it never seemed to be in the professional theatre. After the performance, the floor was cleared for dancing, and the audience were in a mood of thorough enjoyment.

The pageant of the "World Commune," which was performed at the opening of the Third International Congress in Petrograd, was a still more important and significant phenomenon. I do not suppose that anything of the kind has been staged since the days of the mediæval mystery plays. It was, in fact, a mystery play designed by the High Priests of the Communist faith to instruct the people. It was played on the steps of an immense white building that was once the Stock Exchange, a building with a classical colonnade on three sides of it, with a vast flight of steps in front, that did not extend the whole width of the building but left at each side a platform that was level with the floor of the colonnade. In front of this building a wide road ran from a bridge over one arm of the river to a bridge over the other, so that the stretches of water and sky on either side seemed to the eye of imagination like the painted wings of a gigantic stage. Two battered red columns of fantastic design, that were once light towers to guide ships, stood on either side midway between the extremities of the building and the water, but on the opposite side of the road. These two towers were beflagged and illuminated and carried the limelight, and between and behind them was gathered a densely packed audience of forty or fifty thousand people. The play began at sundown, while the sky was still red away to the right and the palaces on the far bank to the left still aglow with the setting sun, and it continued under the magic of the darkening sky. At first the beauty and grandeur of the setting drew the attention away from the performers, but gradually one became aware that on the platform before the columns kings and queens and courtiers in sumptuous conventional robes, and attended by soldiers, were conversing in dumb show with one another. A few climbed the steps of a small wooden platform that was set up in the middle, and one indicated by a lifted hand that here should be built a monument to the power of capitalism over the earth. All gave signs of delight. Sentimental music was heard, and the gay company fell to waltzing away the hours. Meanwhile, from below on the road level, there streamed out of the darkness on either side of the building and up the half-lit steps, their fetters ringing in harmony with the music, the enslaved and toiling masses coming in response to command to build the monument for their masters. It is impossible to describe the exquisite beauty of the slow movement of those dark figures aslant the broad flight of steps; individual expressions were of course indistinguishable, and yet the movement and attitude of the groups conveyed pathos and patient endurance as well as any individual speech or gesture in the ordinary theatre. Some groups carried hammer and anvil, and others staggered under enormous blocks of stone. Love for the ballet has perhaps made the Russians understand the art of moving groups of actors in unison. As I watched these processions climbing the steps in apparently careless and spontaneous fashion, and yet producing so graceful a result, I remembered the mad leap of the archers down the stage in *Prince Igor*, which is also apparently careless and spontaneous and full of wild and irregular beauty, yet never varies a hair-breadth from one performance to the next.

For a time the workers toiled in the shadow in their earthly world, and dancing continued in the lighted paradise of the rulers above, until presently, in sign that the monument was complete, a large yellow disc was hoisted amid acclamation above the highest platform between the columns. But at the same moment a banner was uplifted amongst the people, and a small figure was seen gesticulating. Angry fists were shaken and the banner and speaker disappeared, only to reappear almost immediately in another part of the dense crowd. Again hostility, until finally among the French workers away up on the right, the first Communist manifesto found favour. Rallying around their banner the *communards* ran shouting down the steps, gathering supporters as they came. Above, all is confusion, kings and queens scuttling in unroyal fashion with flying velvet robes to safe citadels right and left, while the army prepares to defend the main citadel of capitalism with its golden disc of power. The *communards* scale the steps to the fortress which they finally capture, haul down the disc and set their banner in its place. The merry music of the *Carmagnole* is heard, and the victors are seen expressing their delight by dancing first on one foot and then on the other, like marionettes. Below, the masses dance with them in a frenzy of joy. But a pompous procession of Prussian legions is seen approaching, and, amid shrieks and wails of despair, the people are driven back, and their leaders set in a row and shot. Thereafter came one of the most moving scenes in the drama. Several dark-clad women appeared carrying a black pall supported on sticks, which they set in front of the bodies of the leaders so that it stood out, an irregular pointed black shape against the white columns behind. But for this melancholy monument the stage was now empty. Thick clouds of black smoke arose from braziers on either side and obscured the steps and the platform. Through the smoke came the distant sound of Chopin's *Marche Funèbre*, and as the air became clearer white figures could be dimly seen moving around the black pall in a solemn dance of mourning. Behind them the columns shone ghostly and unreal against the glimmering mauve rays of an uncertain and watery dawn.

The second part of the pageant opened in July 1914. Once again the rulers were feasting and the workers at toil, but the scene was enlivened by the presence of the leaders of the Second International, a group of decrepit professorial old men, who waddled in in solemn procession carrying tomes full of international learning. They sat in a row between the rulers and the people, deep in study, spectacles on nose. The call to war was the signal for a dramatic appeal from the workers to these leaders, who refused to accept the Red Flag, but weakly received patriotic flags from their respective governments. Jaurès, elevated to be the symbol of protest, towered above the people, crying in a loud voice, but fell back immediately as the assassin's shot rang out. Then the people divided into their national groups and the war began. It was at this point that "God Save the King" was played as the English soldiers marched out, in a comic manner which made one think of it as "*Gawd* save the King." Other national anthems were burlesqued in a similar fashion, but none quite so successfully. A ridiculous effigy of the Tsar with a knout in his hand now occupied the symbolic position and dominated the scene. The incidents of the war which affected Russia were then played. Spectacular cavalry charges on the road, marching soldiers, batteries of artillery, a pathetic procession of cripples and nurses, and other scenes too numerous to describe, made up that part of the pageant devoted to the war.

Then came the Russian Revolution in all its stages. Cars dashed by full of armed men, red flags appeared everywhere, the people stormed the citadel and hauled down the effigy of the Tsar. The Kerensky Government assumed control and drove them forth to war again, but soon they returned to the charge, destroyed the Provisional Government, and hoisted all the emblems of the Russian Soviet Republic. The Entente leaders, however, were seen preparing their troops for battle, and the pageant went on to show the formation of the Red Army under its emblem the Red Star. White figures with golden trumpets appeared foretelling victory for the proletariat. The last scene, the World Commune, is described in the words of the abstract, taken from a Russian newspaper, as follows:—

Cannon shots announce the breaking of the blockade against Soviet Russia, and the victory of the World Proletariat. The Red Army returns from the front, and passes in triumphant review before the leaders of the Revolution. At their feet lie the crowns of kings and the gold of the bankers. Ships draped with flags are seen carrying workers from the west. The workers of the whole world, with the emblems of labour, gather for the celebration of the World Commune. In the heavens luminous inscriptions in different languages appear, greeting the Congress: "Long live the Third International! Workers of the world, unite! Triumph to the sounds of the hymn of the World Commune, the 'International'."

Even so glowing an account, however, hardly does it justice. It had the pomp and majesty of the Day of Judgment itself. Rockets climbed the skies and peppered them with a thousand stars, fireworks blazed on all sides, garlanded and beflagged ships moved up and down the river, chariots bearing the emblems of prosperity, grapes and corn, travelled slowly along the road. The Eastern peoples came carrying gifts and emblems. The actors, massed upon the steps, waved triumphant hands, trumpets sounded, and the song of the International from ten thousand throats rose like a mighty wave engulfing the whole.

Though the end of this drama may have erred on the side of the grandiose, this may perhaps be forgiven the organizers in view of the occasion for which they prepared it. Nothing, however, could detract from the beauty and dramatic power of the opening and of many of the scenes. Moreover, the effects obtained by movement in the mass were almost intoxicating. The first entrance of the masses gave a sense of dumb and patient force that was moving in the extreme, and the frenzied delight of the dancing crowd at the victory of the French *communards* stirred one to ecstasy. The pageant lasted for five hours or more, and was as exhausting emotionally as the Passion Play is said to be. I had the vision of a great period of Communist art, more especially of such open-air spectacles, which should have the grandeur and scope and eternal meaning of the plays of ancient Greece, the mediæval mysteries, or the Shakespearean theatre. In building, writing, acting, even in painting, work would be done, as it once was, by groups, not by one hand or mind, and evolution would proceed slowly until once again the individual emerged from the mass.

In considering Education under the Bolshevik régime, the same two factors which I have already dealt with in discussing art, namely industrial development and the communist doctrine, must be taken into account. Industrial development is in reality one of the tenets of Communism, but as it is one which in Russia is likely to endanger the doctrine as a whole I have thought it better to consider it as a separate item.

As in the matter of art, so in education, those who have given unqualified praise seem to have taken the short and superficial view. It is hardly necessary to launch into descriptions of the crèches, country homes or palaces for children, where Montessori methods prevail, where the pupils cultivate their little gardens, model in plasticine, draw and sing and act, and dance their Eurythmic dances barefoot on floors once sacred to the tread of the nobility. I saw a reception and distributing house in Petrograd with which no fault could be found from the point of view of scientific organization. The children were bright-eyed and merry, and the rooms airy and clean. I saw, too, a performance by school children in Moscow which included some quite wonderful Eurythmic dancing, in particular an interpretation of Grieg's *Tanz in der Halle des Bergkönigs* by the Dalcroze method, but with a colour and warmth which were Russian, and in odd contrast to the mathematical precision associated with most Dalcroze performances.

But in spite of the obvious merit of such institutions as exist, misgivings would arise. To begin with, it must be remembered that it is necessary first to admit that children should be delivered up almost entirely to the State. Nominally, the mother still comes to see her child in these schools, but in actual fact, the drafting of children to the country must intervene, and the whole temper of the authorities seemed to be directed towards breaking the link between mother and child. To some this will seem an advantage, and it is a point which admits of lengthy discussion, but as it belongs rather to the question of women and the family under Communism, I can do no more than mention it here.

Then, again, it must be remembered that the tactics of the Bolsheviks towards such schools as existed under the old régime in provincial towns and villages, have not been the same as their tactics towards the theatres. The greater number of these schools are closed, in part, it would seem, from lack of personnel, and in part from fear of counter-revolutionary propaganda. The result is that, though those schools which they have created are good and organized on modern lines, on the whole there would seem to be less diffusion of child education than before. In this, as in most other departments, the Bolsheviks show themselves loath to attempt anything which cannot be done on a large scale and impregnated with Communist doctrine. It goes without saying that Communist doctrine is taught in schools, as Christianity has been taught hitherto, moreover the Communist teachers show bitter hostility to other teachers who do not accept the doctrine. At the children's entertainment alluded to above, the dances and poems performed had nearly all some close relation to Communism, and a teacher addressed the children for something like an hour and a half on the duties of Communists and the errors of Anarchism.

This teaching of Communism, however necessary it may appear for the building of the Communist state of the future, does seem to me to be an evil in that it is done emotionally and fanatically, with an appeal to hate and militant ardour rather than to constructive reason. It binds the free intellect and destroys initiative. An industrial state needs not only obedient and patient workers and artists, it needs also men and women with initiative in scientific research. It is idle to provide channels for scientific research later if it is to be choked at the source. That source is an enquiring and free intellect unhampered by iron dogma. Beneficial to artistic and emotional development therefore, the teaching of Communism as a faith may well be most pernicious to the scientific and intellectual side of education, and will lead direct to the pragmatist view of knowledge and scientific research which the Church and the capitalist already find it so convenient to adopt.

But to come to the chief and most practical question, the relation of education to industry. Sooner or later education in Russia must become subordinate to the needs of industrial development. That the Bolsheviks already realize this is proved by the articles of Lunacharsky which recently appeared in *Le Phare* (Geneva). It was the spectre of industry that haunted me throughout the consideration of education as in the consideration of art, and what I have said above of its dangers to the latter seems to me also to apply here. Montessori schools belong, in my view, to that stage in industrial development when education is directed as much towards leisure occupations as towards preparation for professional life. Possibly the fine flower of useless scientific enquiry belongs to this stage also. Nobody in Russia is likely to have much leisure for a good many years to come, if the Bolshevik programme of industrial development is efficiently carried out. And there seemed to me to be something pathetic and almost cruel in this varied and agreeable education of the child, when one reflected on the long hours of grinding toil to which he was soon to be subject in workshop or factory. For I repeat that I do not believe industrial work in the early days of industry can be made tolerable to the worker. Once again I experienced the dread of seeing the ideals of the Russian revolutionaries go down before the logic of necessity. They are beginning to pride themselves on being hard, practical men, and it seems quite reasonable to fear that they should come to regard this full and humane development of the child as a mere luxury and ultimately neglect it. Worse still, the few of these schools which already exist may perhaps become exclusive to the Communists and their children, or that company of Samurai which is to leaven and govern the mass of the people. If so, they will soon come to resemble our public schools, in that they will prepare, in an artificial play atmosphere, men who will pass straight to the position of leaders, while the portion of the proletariat who serve under them will be reading and writing, just so much technical training as is necessary, and Communist doctrine.

This is a nightmare hypothesis, but the difficulties of the practical problem seem to warrant its entertainment. The number of people in Russia who can even read and write is extremely small, the need to get them employed industrially as rapidly as possible is very great, hence the system of education which develops out of this situation cannot be very ambitious or enlightened. Further it will have to continue over a sufficiently long period of time to allow of the risk of its becoming stable and traditional. In adult education already the pupil comes for a short period, learns Communism, reading and writing—there is hardly time to give him much more—and returns to leaven the army or his native village. In achieving this the Bolsheviks are already doing a very important and valuable work, but they cannot hope for a long while to become the model of public instruction which they have hitherto been represented to be. And the conditions of their becoming so ultimately are adherence to their ideals through a very long period of stress, and a lessening of fanaticism in their Communist teaching, conditions which, unhappily, seem to be mutually incompatible.

The whole of the argument set out in this chapter may be summed up in the statement of one fact which the mere idealist is prone to overlook, namely that Russia is a country at a stage in economic development not much more advanced than America in the pioneer days. The old civilization was aristocratic and exotic; it could not survive in the modern world. It is true that it produced great men, but its foundations were rotten. The new civilization may, for the moment, be less productive of individual works of genius, but it has a new solidity and gives promise of a new unity. It may be that I have taken too hopeful a view and that the future evolution of Russia will have as little connection with the life and tradition of its present population as modern America with the life of the Red Indian tribes. The fact that there exists in Russia a population at a far higher stage of culture, which will be industrially educated, not exterminated, militates against this hypothesis, but the need for education may make progress slower than it was in the United States.

One would not have looked for the millennium of Communism, nor even for valuable art and educational experiment in the America of early railroading and farming days. Nor must one look for such things from Russia yet. It may be that during the next hundred years there, economic evolution will obscure Communist ideals, until finally, in a country that has reached the stage of present-day America, the battle will be fought out again to a victorious and stable issue. Unless, indeed, the Marxian scripture prove to be not infallible, and faith and heroic devotion show themselves capable of triumphing over economic necessity.

V
COMMUNISM AND THE SOVIET CONSTITUTION

Before I went to Russia I imagined that I was going to see an interesting experiment in a new form of representative government. I did see an interesting experiment, but not in representative government. Every one who is interested in Bolshevism knows the series of elections, from the village meeting to the All-Russian Soviet, by which the people's commissaries are supposed to derive their power. We were told that, by the recall, the occupational constituencies, and so on, a new and far more perfect machinery had been devised for ascertaining and registering the popular will. One of the things we hoped to study was the question whether the Soviet system is really superior to Parliamentarism in this respect.

We were not able to make any such study, because the Soviet system is moribund. No conceivable system of free election would give majorities to the Communists, either in town or country. Various methods are therefore adopted for giving the victory to Government candidates. In the first place, the voting is by show of hands, so that all who vote against the Government are marked men. In the second place, no candidate who is not a Communist can have any printing done, the printing works being all in the hands of the State. In the third place, he cannot address any meetings, because the halls all belong to the State. The whole of the press is, of course, official; no independent daily is permitted. In spite of all these obstacles, the Mensheviks have succeeded in winning about 40 seats out of 1,500 on the Moscow Soviet, by being known in certain large factories where the electoral campaign could be conducted by word of mouth. They won, in fact, every seat that they contested.

But although the Moscow Soviet is nominally sovereign in Moscow, it is really only a body of electors who choose the executive committee of forty, out of which, in turn, is chosen the Presidium, consisting of nine men who have all the power. The Moscow Soviet, as a whole, meets rarely; the Executive Committee is supposed to meet once a week, but did not meet while we were in Moscow. The Presidium, on the contrary, meets daily. Of course, it is easy for the Government to exercise pressure over the election of the executive committee, and again over the election of the Presidium. It must be remembered that effective protest is impossible, owing to the absolutely complete suppression of free speech and free Press. The result is that the Presidium of the Moscow Soviet consists only of orthodox Communists.

Kamenev, the President of the Moscow Soviet, informed us that the recall is very frequently employed; he said that in Moscow there are, on an average, thirty recalls a month. I asked him what were the principal reasons for the recall, and he mentioned four: drinking, going to the front (and being, therefore, incapable of performing the duties), change of politics on the part of the electors, and failure to make a report to the electors once a fortnight, which all members of the Soviet are expected to do. It is evident that the recall affords opportunities for governmental pressure, but I had no chance of finding out whether it is used for this purpose.

In country districts the method employed is somewhat different. It is impossible to secure that the village Soviet shall consist of Communists, because, as a rule, at any rate in the villages I saw, there are no Communists. But when I asked in the villages how they were represented on the Volost (the next larger area) or the Gubernia, I was met always with the reply that they were not represented at all. I could not verify this, and it is probably an overstatement, but all concurred in the assertion that if they elected a non-Communist representative he could not obtain a pass on the railway and, therefore, could not attend the Volost or Gubernia Soviet. I saw a meeting of the Gubernia Soviet of Saratov. The representation is so arranged that the town workers have an enormous preponderance over the surrounding peasants; but even allowing for this, the proportion of peasants seemed astonishingly small for the centre of a very important agricultural area.

The All-Russian Soviet, which is constitutionally the supreme body, to which the People's Commissaries are responsible, meets seldom, and has become increasingly formal. Its sole function at present, so far as I could discover, is to ratify, without discussion, previous decisions of the Communist Party on matters (especially concerning foreign policy) upon which the constitution requires its decision.

All real power is in the hands of the Communist Party, who number about 600,000 in a population of about 120 millions. I never came across a Communist by chance: the people whom I met in the streets or in the villages, when I could get into conversation with them, almost invariably said they were of no party. The only other answer I ever had was from some of the peasants, who openly stated that they were Tsarists. It must be said that the peasants' reasons for disliking the Bolsheviks are very inadequate. It is said—and all I saw confirmed the assertion—that the peasants are better off than they ever were before. I saw no one—man, woman, or child—who looked underfed in the villages. The big landowners are dispossessed, and the peasants have profited. But the towns and the army still need nourishing, and the Government has nothing to give the peasants in return for food except paper, which the peasants resent having to take. It is a singular fact that Tsarist roubles are worth ten times as much as Soviet roubles, and are much commoner in the country. Although they are illegal, pocket-books full of them are openly displayed in the market places. I do not think it should be inferred that the peasants expect a Tsarist restoration: they are merely actuated by custom and dislike of novelty. They have never heard of the blockade; consequently they cannot understand why the Government is unable to give them the clothes and agricultural implements that they need. Having got their land, and being ignorant of affairs outside their own neighbourhood, they wish their own village to be independent, and would resent the demands of any Government whatever.

Within the Communist Party there are, of course, as always in a bureaucracy, different factions, though hitherto the external pressure has prevented disunion. It seemed to me that the personnel of the bureaucracy could be divided into three classes. There are first the old revolutionists, tested by years of persecution. These men have most of the highest posts. Prison and exile have made them tough and fanatical and rather out of touch with their own country. They are honest men, with a profound belief that Communism will regenerate the world. They think themselves utterly free from sentiment, but, in fact, they are sentimental about Communism and about the régime that they are creating; they cannot face the fact that what they are creating is not complete Communism, and that Communism is anathema to the peasant, who wants his own land and nothing else. They are pitiless in punishing corruption or drunkenness when they find either among officials; but they have built up a system in which the temptations to petty corruption are tremendous, and their own materialistic theory should persuade them that under such a system corruption must be rampant.

The second class in the bureaucracy, among whom are to be found most of the men occupying political posts just below the top, consists of *arrivistes*, who are enthusiastic Bolsheviks because of the material success of Bolshevism. With them must be reckoned the army of policemen, spies, and secret agents, largely inherited from the Tsarist times, who make their profit out of the fact that no one can live except by breaking the law. This aspect of Bolshevism is exemplified by the Extraordinary Commission, a body practically independent of the Government, possessing its own regiments, who are better fed than the Red Army. This body has the power of imprisoning any man or woman without trial on such charges as speculation or counter-revolutionary activity. It has shot thousands without proper trial, and though now it has nominally lost the power of inflicting the death penalty, it is by no means certain that it has altogether lost it in fact. It has spies everywhere, and ordinary mortals live in terror of it.

The third class in the bureaucracy consists of men who are not ardent Communists, who have rallied to the Government since it has proved itself stable, and who work for it either out of patriotism or because they enjoy the opportunity of developing their ideas freely without the obstacle of traditional institutions. Among this class are to be found men of the type of the successful business man, men with the same sort of ability as is found in the American self-made Trust magnate, but working for success and power, not for money. There is no doubt that the Bolsheviks are successfully solving the problem of enlisting this kind of ability in the public service, without permitting it to amass wealth as it does in capitalist communities. This is perhaps their greatest success so far, outside the domain of war. It makes it possible to suppose that, if Russia is allowed to have peace, an amazing industrial development may take place, making Russia a rival of the United States. The Bolsheviks are industrialists in all their aims; they love everything in modern industry except the excessive rewards of the capitalists. And the harsh discipline to which they are subjecting the workers is calculated, if anything can, to give them the habits of industry and honesty which have hitherto been lacking, and the lack of which alone prevents Russia from being one of the foremost industrial countries.

FOOTNOTES:

In *Theses* (p. 6 of French edition) it is said: "The ancient classic subdivision of the Labour movement into three forms (parties, trade unions, and co-operatives) has served its time. The proletarian revolution has raised up in Russia the essential form of proletarian dictatorship, the *soviets*. But the work in the Soviets, as in the industrial trade unions which have become revolutionary, must be invariably and systematically directed by the party of the proletariat, i.e. the Communist Party. As the organized advanced guard of the working class, the Communist Party answers equally to the economic, political and spiritual needs of the entire working class. It must be the soul of the trade unions, the soviets, and all other proletarian organizations.

"The appearance of the Soviets, the principal historical form of the dictatorship of the proletariat, in no way diminishes the directing rôle of the party in the proletarian revolution. When the German Communists of the 'Left' ... declare that 'the party itself must also adapt itself more and more to the Soviet idea and proletarianize itself,' we see there only an insinuating expression of the idea that the Communist Party must dissolve itself into the Soviets, so that the Soviets can replace it.

"This idea is profoundly erroneous and reactionary.

"The history of the Russian Revolution shows us, at a certain moment, the Soviets going against the proletarian party and helping the agents of the bourgeoisie....

"In order that the Soviets may fulfil their historic mission, the existence of a Communist Party, strong enough not to 'adapt' itself to the Soviets but to exercise on them a decisive influence, to force them *not to adapt themselves* to the bourgeoisie and official social democracy, ... is on the contrary necessary."

VI
THE FAILURE OF RUSSIAN INDUSTRY

At first sight it is surprising that Russian industry should have collapsed as badly as it has done, and still more surprising that the efforts of the Communists have not been more successful in reviving it. As I believe that the continued efficiency of industry is the main condition for success in the transition to a Communist State, I shall endeavour to analyse the causes of the collapse, with a view to the discovery of ways by which it can be avoided elsewhere.

Of the fact of the collapse there can be no doubt. The Ninth Congress of the Communist Party (March-April, 1920) speaks of "the incredible catastrophes of public economy," and in connection with transport, which is one of the vital elements of the problem, it acknowledges "the terrible collapse of the transport and the railway system," and urges the introduction of "measures which cannot be delayed and which are to obviate the complete paralysis of the railway system and, together with this, the ruin of the Soviet Republic." Almost all those who have visited Russia would confirm this view of the gravity of the situation. In the factories, in great works like those of Putilov and Sornovo, very little except war work is being done; machinery stands idle and plant is becoming unusable. One sees hardly any new manufactured articles in Russia, beyond a certain very inadequate quantity of clothes and boots—always excepting what is needed for the army. And the difficulty of obtaining food is conclusive evidence of the absence of goods such as are needed by the peasants.

How has this state of affairs arisen? And why does it continue?

A great deal of disorganization occurred before the first revolution and under Kerensky. Russian industry was partly dependent on Poland; the war was conducted by methods of reckless extravagance, especially as regards rolling-stock; under Kerensky there was a tendency to universal holiday, under the impression that freedom had removed the necessity for work. But when all this is admitted to the full, it remains true that the state of industry under the Bolsheviks is much worse than even under Kerensky.

The first and most obvious reason for this is that Russia was quite unusually dependent upon foreign assistance. Not only did the machinery in the factories and the locomotives on the railways come from abroad, but the organizing and technical brains in industry were mainly foreign. When the Entente became hostile to Russia, the foreigners in Russian industry either left the country or assisted counter-revolution. Even those who were in fact loyal naturally became suspect, and could not well be employed in responsible posts, any more than Germans could in England during the war. The native Russians who had technical or business skill were little better; they almost all practised sabotage in the first period of the Bolshevik régime. One hears amusing stories of common sailors frantically struggling with complicated accounts, because no competent accountant would work for the Bolsheviks.

But those days passed. When the Government was seen to be stable, a great many of those who had formerly sabotaged it became willing to accept posts under it, and are now in fact so employed, often at quite exceptional salaries. Their importance is thoroughly realized. One resolution at the above-mentioned Congress says (I quote verbally the unedited document which was given to us in Moscow):

Being of opinion that without a scientific organization of industry, even the widest application of compulsory labour service, as the great labour heroism of the working class, will not only fail to secure the establishment of a powerful socialist production, but will also fail to assist the country to free itself from the clutches of poverty—the Congress considers it imperative to register all able specialists of the various departments of public economy and widely to utilize them for the purpose of industrial organization.

The Congress considers the elucidation for the wide masses of the workers of the tremendous character of the economic problems of the country to be one of the chief problems of industrial and general political agitation and propaganda; and of equal importance to this, technical education, and administrative and scientific technical experience. The Congress makes it obligatory on all the members of the party mercilessly to fight that particular obnoxious form, the ignorant conceit which deems the working class capable of solving all problems without the assistance *in the most responsible cases* of specialists of the bourgeois school, the management. Demagogic elements who speculate on this kind of prejudice in the more backward section of our working classes, can have no place in the ranks of the party of Scientific Socialism.

But Russia alone is unable to supply the amount of skill required, and is very deficient in technical instructors, as well as in skilled workmen. One was told, over and over again, that the first step in improvement would be the obtaining of spare parts for locomotives. It seems strange that these could not be manufactured in Russia. To some extent they can be, and we were shown locomotives which had been repaired on Communist Saturdays. But in the main the machinery for making spare parts is lacking and the skill required for its manufacture does not exist. Thus dependence on the outside world persists, and the blockade continues to do its deadly work of spreading hunger, demoralization and despair.

The food question is intimately bound up with the question of industry. There is a vicious circle, for not only does the absence of manufactured goods cause a food shortage in the towns, but the food shortage, in turn, diminishes the strength of the workers and makes them less able to produce goods. I cannot but think that there has been some mismanagement as regards the food question. For example, in Petrograd many workers have allotments and often work in them for eight hours after an eight hours' day in their regular employment. But the food produced in the allotments is taken for general consumption, not left to each individual producer. This is in accordance with Communist theory, but of course greatly diminishes the incentive to work, and increases the red tape and administrative machinery.

Lack of fuel has been another very grave source of trouble. Before the war coal came mostly from Poland and the Donetz Basin. Poland is lost to Russia, and the Donetz Basin was in the hands of Denikin, who so destroyed the mines before retreating that they are still not in working order. The result is a practically complete absence of coal. Oil, which is equally important in Russia, was also lacking until the recent recovery of Baku. All that I saw on the Volga made me believe that real efficiency has been shown in reorganizing the transport of oil, and doubtless this will do something to revive industry. But the oil used to be worked very largely by Englishmen, and English machinery is much needed for refining it. In the meantime, Russia has had to depend upon wood, which involves immense labour. Most of the houses are not warmed in winter, so that people live in a temperature below freezing-point. Another consequence of lack of fuel was the bursting of water-pipes, so that people in Petrograd, for the most part, have to go down to the Neva to fetch their water—a considerable addition to the labour of an already overworked day.

I find it difficult to believe that, if greater efficiency had existed in the Government, the food and fuel difficulties could not have been considerably alleviated. In spite of the needs of the army, there are still many horses in Russia; I saw troops of thousands of horses on the Volga, which apparently belonged to Kalmuk tribes. By the help of carts and sledges, it ought to be possible, without more labour than is warranted by the importance of the problem, to bring food and timber into Moscow and Petrograd. It must be remembered that both cities are surrounded by forests, and Moscow at least is surrounded by good agricultural land. The Government has devoted all its best energies hitherto to the two tasks of war and propaganda, while industry and the food problem have been left to a lesser degree of energy and intelligence. It is no doubt probable that, if peace is secured, the economic problems will receive more attention than hitherto. But the Russian character seems less adapted to steady work of an unexciting nature than to heroic efforts on great occasions; it has immense passive endurance, but not much active tenacity. Whether, with the menace of foreign invasion removed, enough day-by-day detailed energy would exist for the reorganization of industry, is a doubtful question, as to which only time can decide.

This leads to the conclusion—which I think is adopted by most of the leading men in Russia—that it will be very difficult indeed to save the revolution without outside economic assistance. Outside assistance from capitalist countries is dangerous to the principles of Communism, as well as precarious from the likelihood of fresh causes of quarrel. But the need of help is urgent, and if the policy of promoting revolution elsewhere were to succeed, it would probably render the nations concerned temporarily incapable of supplying Russian needs. It is, therefore, necessary for Russia to accept the risks and uncertainties involved in attempting to make peace with the Entente and to trade with America. By continuing war, Russia can do infinite damage to us, especially in Asia, but cannot hope, for many years, to achieve any degree of internal prosperity. The situation, therefore, is one in which, even from the narrowest point of view, peace is to the interest of both parties.

It is difficult for an outsider with only superficial knowledge to judge of the efforts which have been made to reorganize industry without outside help. These efforts have chiefly taken the form of industrial conscription. Workers in towns seek to escape to the country, in order to have enough to eat; but this is illegal and severely punished. The same Communist Report from which I have already quoted speaks on this subject as follows:

Labour Desertion.—Owing to the fact that a considerable part of the workers either in search of better food conditions or often for the purposes of speculation, voluntarily leave their places of employment or change from place to place, which inevitably harms production and deteriorates the general position of the working class, the Congress considers one of the most urgent problems of Soviet Government and of the Trade Union organization to be established as the firm, systematic and insistent struggle with labour desertion, The way to fight this is to publish a list of desertion fines, the creation of a labour Detachment of Deserters under fine, and, finally, internment in concentration camps.

It is hoped to extend the system to the peasantry:

The defeat of the White Armies and the problems of peaceful construction in connection with the incredible catastrophes of public economy demand an extraordinary effort of all the powers of the proletariat and the drafting into the process of public labour of the wide masses of the peasantry.

On the vital subject of transport, in a passage of which I have already quoted a fragment, the Communist Party declares:

For the most immediate future transport remains the centre of the attention and the efforts of the Soviet Government. The improvement of transport is the indispensable basis upon which even the most moderate success in all other spheres of production and first of all in the provision question can be gained.

The chief difficulty with regard to the improvement of transport is the weakness of the Transport Trade Union, which is due in the first case to the heterogeneity of the personnel of the railways, amongst whom there are still a number of those who belong to the period of disorganization, and, secondly, to the fact that the most class-conscious and best elements of the railway proletariat were at the various fronts of the civil war.

Considering wide Trade Union assistance to the railway workers to be one of the principal tasks of the Party, and as the only condition under which transport can be raised to its height, the Congress at the same time recognizes the inflexible necessity of employing exclusive and extraordinary measures (martial law, and so forth). Such necessity is the result of the terrible collapse of the transport and the railroad system and is to introduce measures which cannot be delayed and which are to obviate the complete paralysis of the railway system and, together with this, the ruin of the Soviet Republic.

The general attitude to the militarization of labour is stated in the Resolution with which this section of the Proceedings begins:

The ninth Congress approves of the decision of the Central Committee of the Russian Communist Party on the mobilization of the industrial proletariat, compulsory labour service, militarization of production and the application of military detachments to economic needs.

In connection with the above, the Congress decrees that the Party organization should in every way assist the Trade Unions and the Labour Sections in registering all skilled workers with a view of employing them in the various branches of production with the same consistency and strictness as was done, and is being carried out at the present time, in relation to the commanding staff for army needs.

Every skilled worker is to return to his particular trade Exceptions, i.e. the retention of the skilled worker in any other branch of Soviet service, is allowed only with the sanction of the corresponding central and local authorities.

It is, of course, evident that in these measures the Bolsheviks have been compelled to travel a long way from the ideals which originally inspired the revolution. But the situation is so desperate that they could not be blamed if their measures were successful. In a shipwreck all hands must turn to, and it would be ridiculous to prate of individual liberty. The most distressing feature of the situation is that these stern laws seem to have produced so little effect. Perhaps in the course of years Russia might become self-supporting without help from the outside world, but the suffering meantime would be terrible. The early hopes of the revolution would fade more and more. Every failure of industry, every tyrannous regulation brought about by the desperate situation, is used by the Entente as a justification of its policy. If a man is deprived of food and drink, he will grow weak, lose his reason, and finally die. This is not usually considered a good reason for inflicting death by starvation. But where nations are concerned, the weakness and struggles are regarded as morally culpable, and are held to justify further punishment. So at least it has been in the case of Russia. Nothing produced a doubt in our governing minds as to the rightness of our policy except the strength of the Red Army and the fear of revolution in Asia. Is it surprising that professions of humanitarian feeling on the part of English people are somewhat coldly received in Soviet Russia?

VII
DAILY LIFE IN MOSCOW

Daily life in Moscow, so far as I could discover, has neither the horrors depicted by the Northcliffe Press nor the delights imagined by the more ardent of our younger Socialists.

On the one hand, there is no disorder, very little crime, not much insecurity for those who keep clear of politics. Everybody works hard; the educated people have, by this time, mostly found their way into Government offices or teaching or some other administrative profession in which their education is useful. The theatres, the opera and the ballet continue as before, and are quite admirable; some of the seats are paid for, others are given free to members of trade unions. There is, of course, no drunkenness, or at any rate so little that none of us ever saw a sign of it. There is very little prostitution, infinitely less than in any other capital. Women are safer from molestation than anywhere else in the world. The whole impression is one of virtuous, well-ordered activity.

On the other hand, life is very hard for all except men in good posts. It is hard, first of all, owing to the food shortage. This is familiar to all who have interested themselves in Russia, and it is unnecessary to dwell upon it. What is less realized is that most people work much longer hours than in this country. The eight-hour day was introduced with a flourish of trumpets; then, owing to the pressure of the war, it was extended to ten hours in certain trades. But no provision exists against extra work at other jobs, and very many people do extra work, because the official rates do not afford a living wage. This is not the fault of the Government, at any rate as regards the major part; it is due chiefly to war and blockade. When the day's work is over, a great deal of time has to be spent in fetching food and water and other necessaries of life. The sight of the workers going to and fro, shabbily clad, with the inevitable bundle in one hand and tin can in the other, through streets almost entirely empty of traffic, produces the effect of life in some vast village, rather than in an important capital city.

Holidays, such as are common throughout all but the very poorest class in this country, are very difficult in Russia. A train journey requires a permit, which is only granted on good reasons being shown; with the present shortage of transport, this regulation is quite unavoidable. Railway queues are a common feature in Moscow; it often takes several days to get a permit. Then, when it has been obtained, it may take several more days to get a seat in a train. The ordinary trains are inconceivably crowded, far more so, though that seems impossible, than London trains at the busiest hour. On the shorter journeys, passengers are even known to ride on the roof and buffers, or cling like flies to the sides of the waggons. People in Moscow travel to the country whenever they can afford the time and get a permit, because in the country there is enough to eat. They go to stay with relations—most people in Moscow, in all classes, but especially among manual workers, have relations in the country. One cannot, of course, go to an hotel as one would in other countries. Hotels have been taken over by the State, and the rooms in them (when they are still used) are allocated by the police to people whose business is recognized as important by the authorities. Casual travel is therefore impossible even on a holiday.

Journeys have vexations in addition to the slowness and overcrowding of the trains. Police search the travellers for evidences of "speculation," especially for food. The police play, altogether, a much greater part in daily life than they do in other countries—much greater than they did, for example, in Prussia twenty-five years ago, when there was a vigorous campaign against Socialism. Everybody breaks the law almost daily, and no one knows which among his acquaintances is a spy of the Extraordinary Commission. Even in the prisons, among prisoners, there are spies, who are allowed certain privileges but not their liberty.

Newspapers are not taken in, except by very few people, but they are stuck up in public places, where passers-by occasionally glance at them. There is very little to read; owing to paper shortage, books are rare, and money to buy them is still rarer. One does not see people reading, as one does here in the Underground for example. There is practically no social life, partly because of the food shortage, partly because, when anybody is arrested, the police are apt to arrest everybody whom they find in his company, or who comes to visit him. And once arrested, a man or woman, however innocent, may remain for months in prison without trial. While we were in Moscow, forty social revolutionaries and Anarchists were hunger-striking to enforce their demand to be tried and to be allowed visits. I was told that on the eighth day of the strike the Government consented to try them, and that few could be proved guilty of any crime; but I had no means of verifying this.

Industrial conscription is, of course, rigidly enforced. Every man and woman has to work, and slacking is severely punished, by prison or a penal settlement. Strikes are illegal, though they sometimes occur. By proclaiming itself the friend of the proletarian, the Government has been enabled to establish an iron discipline, beyond the wildest dreams of the most autocratic American magnate. And by the same professions the Government has led Socialists from other countries to abstain from reporting unpleasant features in what they have seen.

The Tolstoyans, of whom I saw the leaders, are obliged by their creed to resist every form of conscription, though some have found ways of compromising. The law concerning conscientious objectors to military service is practically the same as ours, and its working depends upon the temper of the tribunal before which a man comes. Some conscientious objectors have been shot; on the other hand, some have obtained absolute exemption.

Life in Moscow, as compared to life in London, is drab, monotonous, and depressed. I am not, of course, comparing life there with that of the rich here, but with that of the average working-class family. When it is realized that the highest wages are about fifteen shillings a month, this is not surprising. I do not think that life could, under any system, be very cheerful in a country so exhausted by war as Russia, so I am not saying this as a criticism of the Bolsheviks. But I do think there might be less police interference, less vexatious regulation, and more freedom for spontaneous impulses towards harmless enjoyments.

Religion is still very strong. I went into many churches, where I saw obviously famished priests in gorgeous vestments, and a congregation enormously devout. Generally more than half the congregation were men, and among the men many were soldiers. This applies to the towns as well as to the country. In Moscow I constantly saw people in the streets crossing themselves.

There is a theory that the Moscow working man feels himself free from capitalist domination, and therefore bears hardships gladly. This is no doubt true of the minority who are active Communists, but I do not think it has any truth for the others. The average working man, to judge by a rather hasty impression, feels himself the slave of the Government, and has no sense whatever of having been liberated from a tyranny.

I recognize to the full the reasons for the bad state of affairs, in the past history of Russia and the recent policy of the Entente. But I have thought it better to record impressions frankly, trusting the readers to remember that the Bolsheviks have only a very limited share of responsibility for the evils from which Russia is suffering.

FOOTNOTES:

The ninth Communist Congress (March-April, 1920) says on this subject: "In view of the fact that the first condition of the success of the

Soviet Republic in all departments, including the economic, is chiefly systematic printed agitation, the Congress draws the attention of the Soviet Government to the deplorable state in which our paper and printing industries find themselves. The ever decreasing number of newspapers fail to reach not only the peasants but even the workers, in addition to which our poor technical means render the papers hardly readable. The Congress strongly appeals to the Supreme Council of Public Economy, to the corresponding Trade Unions and other interested institutions, to apply all efforts to raise the quantity, to introduce general system and order in the printing business, and so secure for the worker and peasant in Russia a supply of Socialist printed matter."

VIIIToC
TOWN AND COUNTRY

The problem of inducing the peasants to feed the towns is one which Russia shares with Central Europe, and from what one hears Russia has been less unsuccessful than some other countries in dealing with this problem. For the Soviet Government, the problem is mainly concentrated in Moscow and Petrograd; the other towns are not very large, and are mostly in the centre of rich agricultural districts. It is true that in the North even the rural population normally depends upon food from more southerly districts; but the northern population is small. It is commonly said that the problem of feeding Moscow and Petrograd is a transport problem, but I think this is only partially true. There is, of course, a grave deficiency of rolling-stock, especially of locomotives in good repair. But Moscow is surrounded by very good land. In the course of a day's motoring in the neighbourhood, I saw enough cows to supply milk to the whole child population of Moscow, although what I had come to see was children's sanatoria, not farms. All kinds of food can be bought in the market at high prices. I travelled over a considerable extent of Russian railways, and saw a fair number of goods trains. For all these reasons, I feel convinced that the share of the transport problem in the food difficulties has been exaggerated. Of course transport plays a larger part in the shortage in Petrograd than in Moscow, because food comes mainly from south of Moscow. In Petrograd, most of the people one sees in the streets show obvious signs of under-feeding. In Moscow, the visible signs are much less frequent, but there is no doubt that under-feeding, though not actual starvation, is nearly universal.

The Government supplies rations to every one who works in the towns at a very low fixed price. The official theory is that the Government has a monopoly of the food and that the rations are sufficient to sustain life. The fact is that the rations are not sufficient, and that they are only a portion of the food supply of Moscow. Moreover, people complain, I do not know how truly, that the rations are delivered irregularly; some say, about every other day. Under these circumstances, almost everybody, rich or poor, buys food in the market, where it costs about fifty times the fixed Government price. A pound of butter costs about a month's wages. In order to be able to afford extra food, people adopt various expedients. Some do additional work, at extra rates, after their official day's work is over. For, though there is supposed to be by law an eight-hours day, extended to ten in certain vital industries, the wage paid for it is not a living wage, and there is nothing to prevent a man from undertaking other work in his spare time. But the usual resource is what is called "speculation," i.e., buying and selling. Some person formerly rich sells clothes or furniture or jewellery in return for food; the buyer sells again at an enhanced price, and so on through perhaps twenty hands, until a final purchaser is found in some well-to-do peasant or *nouveau riche* speculator. Again, most people have relations in the country, whom they visit from time to time, bringing back with them great bags of flour. It is illegal for private persons to bring food into Moscow, and the trains are searched; but, by corruption or cunning, experienced people can elude the search. The food market is illegal, and is raided occasionally; but as a rule it is winked at. Thus the attempt to suppress private commerce has resulted in an amount of unprofessional buying and selling which far exceeds what happens in capitalist countries. It takes up a great deal of time that might be more profitably employed; and, being illegal, it places practically the whole population of Moscow at the mercy of the police. Moreover, it depends largely upon the stores of goods belonging to those who were formerly rich, and when these are expended the whole system must collapse, unless industry has meanwhile been re-established on a sound basis.

It is clear that the state of affairs is unsatisfactory, but, from the Government's point of view, it is not easy to see what ought to be done. The urban and industrial population is mainly concerned in carrying on the work of government and supplying munitions to the army. These are very necessary tasks, the cost of which ought to be defrayed out of taxation. A moderate tax in kind on the peasants would easily feed Moscow and Petrograd. But the peasants take no interest in war or government. Russia is so vast that invasion of one part does not touch another part; and the peasants are too ignorant to have any national consciousness, such as one takes for granted in England or France or Germany. The peasants will not willingly part with a portion of their produce merely for purposes of national defence, but only for the goods they need—clothes, agricultural implements, &c.—which the Government, owing to the war and the blockade, is not in a position to supply.

When the food shortage was at its worst, the Government antagonized the peasants by forced requisitions, carried out with great harshness by the Red Army. This method has been modified, but the peasants still part unwillingly with their food, as is natural in view of the uselessness of paper and the enormously higher prices offered by private buyers.

The food problem is the main cause of popular opposition to the Bolsheviks, yet I cannot see how any popular policy could have been adopted. The Bolsheviks are disliked by the peasants because they take so much food; they are disliked in the towns because they take so little. What the peasants want is what is called free trade, i.e., de-control of agricultural produce. If this policy were adopted, the towns would be faced by utter starvation, not merely by hunger and hardship. It is an entire misconception to suppose that the peasants cherish any hostility to the Entente. The *Daily News* of July 13th, in an otherwise excellent leading article, speaks of "the growing hatred of the Russian peasant, who is neither a Communist nor a Bolshevik, for the Allies generally and this country in particular." The typical Russian peasant has never heard of the Allies or of this country; he does not know that there is a blockade; all he knows is that he used to have six cows but the Government reduced him to one for the sake of poorer peasants, and that it takes his corn (except what is needed for his own family) at a very low price. The reasons for these actions do not interest him, since his horizon is bounded by his own village. To a remarkable extent, each village is an independent unit. So long as the Government obtains the food and soldiers that it requires, it does not interfere, and leaves untouched the old village communism, which is extraordinarily unlike Bolshevism and entirely dependent upon a very primitive stage of culture.

The Government represents the interests of the urban and industrial population, and is, as it were, encamped amid a peasant nation, with whom its relations are rather diplomatic and military than governmental in the ordinary sense. The economic situation, as in Central Europe, is favourable to the country and unfavourable to the towns. If Russia were governed democratically, according to the will of the majority, the inhabitants of Moscow and Petrograd would die of starvation. As it is, Moscow and Petrograd just manage to live, by having the whole civil and military power of the State devoted to their needs. Russia affords the curious spectacle of a vast and powerful Empire, prosperous at the periphery, but faced with dire want at the centre. Those who have least prosperity have most power; and it is only through their excess of power that they are enabled to live at all. The situation is due at bottom to two facts: that almost the whole industrial energies of the population have had to be devoted to war, and that the peasants do not appreciate the importance of the war or the fact of the blockade.

It is futile to blame the Bolsheviks for an unpleasant and difficult situation which it has been impossible for them to avoid. Their problem is only soluble in one of two ways: by the cessation of the war and the blockade, which would enable them to supply the peasants with the goods they need in exchange for food; or by the gradual development of an independent Russian industry. This latter method would be slow, and would involve terrible hardships, but some of the ablest men in the Government believe it to be possible if peace cannot be achieved. If we force this method upon Russia by the refusal of peace and trade, we shall forfeit the only inducement we can hold out for friendly relations; we shall render the Soviet State unassailable and completely free to pursue the policy of promoting revolution everywhere. But the industrial problem is a large subject, which has been already discussed in Chapter VI.

IX
INTERNATIONAL POLICY

In the course of these chapters, I have had occasion to mention disagreeable features of the Bolshevik régime. But it must always be remembered that these are chiefly due to the fact that the industrial life of Russia has been paralysed except as ministering to the wants of the Army, and that the Government has had to wage a bitter and doubtful civil and external war, involving the constant menace of domestic enemies. Harshness, espionage, and a curtailment of liberty result unavoidably from these difficulties. I have no doubt whatever that the sole cure for the evils from which Russia is suffering is peace and trade. Peace and trade would put an end to the hostility of the peasants, and would at once enable the Government to depend upon popularity rather than force. The character of the Government would alter rapidly under such conditions. Industrial conscription, which is now rigidly enforced, would become unnecessary. Those who desire a more liberal spirit would be able to make their voices heard without the feeling that they were assisting reaction and the national enemies. The food difficulties would cease, and with them the need for an autocratic system in the towns.

It must not be assumed, as is common with opponents of Bolshevism, that any other Government could easily be established in Russia. I think every one who has been in Russia recently is convinced that the existing Government is stable. It may undergo internal developments, and might easily, but for Lenin, become a Bonapartist military autocracy. But this would be a change from within—not perhaps a very great change—and would probably do little to alter the economic system. From what I saw of the Russian character and of the opposition parties, I became persuaded that Russia is not ready for any form of democracy, and needs a strong Government. The Bolsheviks represent themselves as the Allies of Western advanced Socialism, and from this point of view they are open to grave criticism. For their international programme there is, to my mind, nothing to be said. But as a national Government, stripped of their camouflage, regarded as the successors of Peter the Great, they are performing a necessary though unamiable task. They are introducing, as far as they can, American efficiency among a lazy and undisciplined population. They are preparing to develop the natural resources of their country by the methods of State Socialism, for which, in Russia, there is much to be said. In the Army they are abolishing illiteracy, and if they had peace they would do great things for education everywhere.

But if we continue to refuse peace and trade, I do not think the Bolsheviks will go under. Russia will endure great hardships, in the years to come as before. But the Russians are inured to misery as no Western nation is; they can live and work under conditions which we should find intolerable. The Government will be driven more and more, from mere self-preservation, into a policy of imperialism. The Entente has been doing everything to expose Germany to a Russian invasion of arms and leaflets, by allowing Poland to engage in war and compelling Germany to disarm. All Asia lies open to Bolshevik ambitions. Almost the whole of the former Russian Empire in Asia is quite firmly in their grasp. Trains are running at a reasonable speed to Turkestan, and I saw cotton from there being loaded on to Volga steamers. In Persia and Turkey, revolts are taking place, with Bolshevik support. It is only a question of a few years before India will be in touch with the Red Army. If we continue to antagonize the Bolsheviks, I do not see what force exists that can prevent them from acquiring the whole of Asia within ten years.

The Russian Government is not yet definitely imperialistic in spirit, and would still prefer peace to conquest. The country is weary of war and denuded of goods. But if the Western Powers insist upon war, another spirit, which is already beginning to show itself, will become dominant. Conquest will be the only alternative to submission. Asiatic conquest will not be difficult. But for us, from the imperialist standpoint, it will mean utter ruin. And for the Continent it will mean revolutions, civil wars, economic cataclysms. The policy of crushing Bolshevism by force was always foolish and criminal; it has now become impossible and fraught with disaster. Our own Government, it would seem, have begun to realize the dangers, but apparently they do not realize them sufficiently to enforce their view against opposition.

In the Theses presented to the Second Congress of the Third International (July 1920), there is a very interesting article by Lenin called "First Sketch of the Theses on National and Colonial Questions" (*Theses*, pp. 40-47). The following passages seemed to me particularly illuminating:—

The present world-situation in politics places on the order of the day the dictatorship of the proletariat; and all the events of world politics are inevitably concentrated round one centre of gravity: the struggle of the international bourgeoisie against the Soviet Republic, which inevitably groups round it, on the one hand the Sovietist movements of the advanced working men of all countries, on the other hand all the national movements of emancipation of colonies and oppressed nations which have been convinced by a bitter experience that there is no salvation for them except in the victory of the Soviet Government over world-imperialism.

We cannot therefore any longer confine ourselves to recognizing and proclaiming the union of the workers of all countries. It is henceforth necessary to pursue the realization of the strictest union of all the national and colonial movements of emancipation with Soviet Russia, by giving to this union forms corresponding to the degree of evolution of the proletarian movement among the proletariat of each country, or of the democratic-bourgeois movement of emancipation among the workers and peasants of backward countries or backward nationalities.

The federal principle appears to us as a transitory form towards the complete unity of the workers of all countries.

This is the formula for co-operation with Sinn Fein or with Egyptian and Indian nationalism. It is further defined later. In regard to backward countries, Lenin says, we must have in view:—

The necessity of the co-operation of all Communists in the democratic-bourgeois movement of emancipation in those countries.

Again:

"The Communist International must conclude temporary alliances with the bourgeois democracy of backward countries, but must never fuse with it." The class-conscious proletariat must "show itself particularly circumspect towards the survivals of national sentiment in countries long oppressed," and must "consent to certain useful concessions."

The Asiatic policy of the Russian Government was adopted as a move against the British Empire, and as a method of inducing the British Government to make peace. It plays a larger part in the schemes of the leading Bolsheviks than is realized by the Labour Party in this country. Its method is not, for the present, to preach Communism, since the Persians and Hindoos are considered scarcely ripe for the doctrines of Marx. It is nationalist movements that are supported by money and agitators from Moscow. The method of quasi-independent states under Bolshevik protection is well understood. It is obvious that this policy affords opportunities for imperialism, under the cover of propaganda, and there is no doubt that some among the Bolsheviks are fascinated by its imperialist aspect. The importance officially attached to the Eastern policy is illustrated by the fact that it was the subject of the concluding portion of Lenin's speech to the recent Congress of the Third International (July 1920).

Bolshevism, like everything Russian, is partly Asiatic in character. One may distinguish two distinct trends, developing into two distinct policies. On the one side are the practical men, who wish to develop Russia industrially, to secure the gains of the Revolution nationally, to trade with the West, and gradually settle down into a more or less ordinary State.

These men have on their side the fact of the economic exhaustion of Russia, the danger of ultimate revolt against Bolshevism if life continues to be as painful as it is at present, and the natural sentiment of humanity that wishes to relieve the sufferings of the people; also the fact that, if revolutions elsewhere produce a similar collapse of industry, they will make it impossible for Russia to receive the outside help which is urgently needed. In the early days, when the Government was weak, they had unchallenged control of policy, but success has made their position less secure.

On the other side there is a blend of two quite different aims: first, the desire to promote revolution in the Western nations, which is in line with Communist theory, and is also thought to be the only way of obtaining a really secure peace; secondly, the desire for Asiatic dominion, which is probably accompanied in the minds of some with dreams of sapphires and rubies and golden thrones and all the glories of their forefather Solomon. This desire produces an unwillingness to abandon the Eastern policy, although it is realized that, until it is abandoned, peace with capitalist England is impossible. I do not know whether there are some to whom the thought occurs that if England were to embark on revolution we should become willing to abandon India to the Russians. But I am certain that the converse thought occurs, namely that, if India could be taken from us, the blow to imperialist feeling might lead us to revolution. In either case, the two policies, of revolution in the West and conquest (disguised as liberation of oppressed peoples) in the East, work in together, and dovetail into a strongly coherent whole.

Bolshevism as a social phenomenon is to be reckoned as a religion, not as an ordinary political movement. The important and effective mental attitudes to the world may be broadly divided into the religious and the scientific. The scientific attitude is tentative and piecemeal, believing what it finds evidence for, and no more. Since Galileo, the scientific attitude has proved itself increasingly capable of ascertaining important facts and laws, which are acknowledged by all competent people regardless of temperament or self-interest or political pressure. Almost all the progress in the world from the earliest times is attributable to science and the scientific temper; almost all the major ills are attributable to religion.

By a religion I mean a set of beliefs held as dogmas, dominating the conduct of life, going beyond or contrary to evidence, and inculcated by methods which are emotional or authoritarian, not intellectual. By this definition, Bolshevism is a religion: that its dogmas go beyond or contrary to evidence, I shall try to prove in what follows. Those who accept Bolshevism become impervious to scientific evidence, and commit intellectual suicide. Even if all the doctrines of Bolshevism were true, this would still be the case, since no unbiased examination of them is tolerated. One who believes, as I do, that the free intellect is the chief engine of human progress, cannot but be fundamentally opposed to Bolshevism, as much as to the Church of Rome.

Among religions, Bolshevism is to be reckoned with Mohammedanism rather than with Christianity and Buddhism. Christianity and Buddhism are primarily personal religions, with mystical doctrines and a love of contemplation. Mohammedanism and Bolshevism are practical, social, unspiritual, concerned to win the empire of this world. Their founders would not have resisted the third of the temptations in the wilderness. What Mohammedanism did for the Arabs, Bolshevism may do for the Russians. As Ali went down before the politicians who only rallied to the Prophet after his success, so the genuine Communists may go down before those who are now rallying to the ranks of the Bolsheviks. If so, Asiatic empire with all its pomps and splendours may well be the next stage of development, and Communism may seem, in historical retrospect, as small a part of Bolshevism as abstinence from alcohol is of Mohammedanism. It is true that, as a world force, whether for revolution or for empire, Bolshevism must sooner or later be brought by success into a desperate conflict with America; and America is more solid and strong, as yet, than anything that Mohammed's followers had to face. But the doctrines of Communism are almost certain, in the long run, to make progress among American wage-earners, and the opposition of America is therefore not likely to be eternal. Bolshevism may go under in Russia, but even if it does it will spring up again elsewhere, since it is ideally suited to an industrial population in distress. What is evil in it is mainly due to the fact that it has its origin in distress; the problem is to disentangle the good from the evil, and induce the adoption of the good in countries not goaded into ferocity by despair.

Russia is a backward country, not yet ready for the methods of equal co-operation which the West is seeking to substitute for arbitrary power in politics and industry. In Russia, the methods of the Bolsheviks are probably more or less unavoidable; at any rate, I am not prepared to criticize them in their broad lines. But they are not the methods appropriate to more advanced countries, and our Socialists will be unnecessarily retrograde if they allow the prestige of the Bolsheviks to lead them into slavish imitation. It will be a far less excusable error in our reactionaries if, by their unteachableness, they compel the adoption of violent methods. We have a heritage of civilization and mutual tolerance which is important to ourselves and to the world. Life in Russia has always been fierce and cruel, to a far greater degree than with us, and out of the war has come a danger that this fierceness and cruelty may become universal. I have hopes that in England this may be avoided through the moderation of both sides. But it is essential to a happy issue that melodrama should no longer determine our views of the Bolsheviks: they are neither angels to be worshipped nor devils to be exterminated, but merely bold and able men attempting with great skill an almost impossible task.

PART II
BOLSHEVIK THEORY

IToC
THE MATERIALISTIC THEORY OF HISTORY

The materialistic conception of history, as it is called, is due to Marx, and underlies the whole Communist philosophy. I do not mean, of course, that a man could not be a Communist without accepting it, but that in fact it is accepted by the Communist Party, and that it profoundly influences their views as to politics and tactics. The name does not convey at all accurately what is meant by the theory. It means that all the mass-phenomena of history are determined by economic motives. This view has no essential connection with materialism in the philosophic sense. Materialism in the philosophic sense may be defined as the theory that all apparently mental occurrences either are really physical, or at any rate have purely physical causes. Materialism in this sense also was preached by Marx, and is accepted by all orthodox Marxians. The arguments for and against it are long and complicated, and need not concern us, since, in fact, its truth or falsehood has little or no bearing on politics.

In particular, philosophic materialism does not prove that economic causes are fundamental in politics. The view of Buckle, for example, according to which climate is one of the decisive factors, is equally compatible with materialism. So is the Freudian view, which traces everything to sex. There are innumerable ways of viewing history which are materialistic in the philosophic sense without being economic or falling within the Marxian formula. Thus the "materialistic conception of history" may be false even if materialism in the philosophic sense should be true.

On the other hand, economic causes might be at the bottom of all political events even if philosophic materialism were false. Economic causes operate through men's desire for possessions, and would be supreme if this desire were supreme, even if desire could not, from a philosophic point of view, be explained in materialistic terms.

There is, therefore, no logical connection either way between philosophic materialism and what is called the "materialistic conception of history."

It is of some moment to realize such facts as this, because otherwise political theories are both supported and opposed for quite irrelevant reasons, and arguments of theoretical philosophy are employed to determine questions which depend upon concrete facts of human nature.

This mixture damages both philosophy and politics, and is therefore important to avoid.

For another reason, also, the attempt to base a political theory upon a philosophical doctrine is undesirable. The philosophical doctrine of materialism, if true at all, is true everywhere and always; we cannot expect exceptions to it, say, in Buddhism or in the Hussite movement. And so it comes about that people whose politics are supposed to be a consequence of their metaphysics grow absolute and sweeping, unable to admit that a general theory of history is likely, at best, to be only true on the whole and in the main. The dogmatic character of Marxian Communism finds support in the supposed philosophic basis of the doctrine; it has the fixed certainty of Catholic theology, not the changing fluidity and sceptical practicality of modern science.

Treated as a practical approximation, not as an exact metaphysical law, the materialistic conception of history has a very large measure of truth. Take, as an instance of its truth, the influence of industrialism upon ideas. It is industrialism, rather than the arguments of Darwinians and Biblical critics, that has led to the decay of religious belief in the urban working class. At the same time, industrialism has revived religious belief among the rich. In the eighteenth century French aristocrats mostly became free-thinkers; now their descendants are mostly Catholics, because it has become necessary for all the forces of reaction to unite against the revolutionary proletariat. Take, again, the emancipation of women. Plato, Mary Wolstonecraft, and John Stuart Mill produced admirable arguments, but influenced only a few impotent idealists. The war came, leading to the employment of women in industry on a large scale, and instantly the arguments in favour of votes for women were seen to be irresistible. More than that, traditional sexual morality collapsed, because its whole basis was the economic dependence of women upon their fathers and husbands. Changes in such a matter as sexual morality bring with them profound alterations in the thoughts and feelings of ordinary men and women; they modify law, literature, art, and all kinds of institutions that seem remote from economics.

Such facts as these justify Marxians in speaking, as they do, of "bourgeois ideology," meaning that kind of morality which has been imposed upon the world by the possessors of capital. Contentment with one's lot may be taken as typical of the virtues preached by the rich to the poor. They honestly believe it is a virtue—at any rate they did formerly. The more religious among the poor also believed it, partly from the influence of authority, partly from an impulse to submission, what MacDougall calls "negative self-feeling," which is commoner than some people think. Similarly men preached the virtue of female chastity, and women usually accepted their teaching; both really believed the doctrine, but its persistence was only possible through the economic power of men. This led erring women to punishment here on earth, which made further punishment hereafter seem probable. When the economic penalty ceased, the conviction of sinfulness gradually decayed. In such changes we see the collapse of "bourgeois ideology."

But in spite of the fundamental importance of economic facts in determining the politics and beliefs of an age or nation, I do not think that non-economic factors can be neglected without risks of errors which may be fatal in practice.

The most obvious non-economic factor, and the one the neglect of which has led Socialists most astray, is nationalism. Of course a nation, once formed, has economic interests which largely determine its politics; but it is not, as a rule, economic motives that decide what group of human beings shall form a nation. Trieste, before the war, considered itself Italian, although its whole prosperity as a port depended upon its belonging to Austria. No economic motive can account for the opposition between Ulster and the rest of Ireland. In Eastern Europe, the Balkanization produced by self-determination has been obviously disastrous from an economic point of view, and was demanded for reasons which were in essence sentimental. Throughout the war wage-earners, with only a few exceptions, allowed themselves to be governed by nationalist feeling, and ignored the traditional Communist exhortation: "Workers of the world, unite." According to Marxian orthodoxy, they were misled by cunning capitalists, who made their profit out of the slaughter. But to any one capable of observing psychological facts, it is obvious that this is largely a myth. Immense numbers of capitalists were ruined by the war; those who were young were just as liable to be killed as the proletarians were. No doubt commercial rivalry between England and Germany had a great deal to do with causing the war; but rivalry is a different thing from profit-seeking. Probably by combination English and German capitalists could have made more than they did out of rivalry, but the rivalry was instinctive, and its economic form was accidental. The capitalists were in the grip of nationalist instinct as much as their proletarian "dupes." In both classes some have gained by the war; but the universal will to war was not produced by the hope of gain. It was produced by a different set of instincts, and one which Marxian psychology fails to recognize adequately.

The Marxian assumes that a man's "herd," from the point of view of herd-instinct, is his class, and that he will combine with those whose economic class-interest is the same as his. This is only very partially true in fact. Religion has been the most decisive factor in determining a man's herd throughout long periods of the world's history. Even now a Catholic working man will vote for a Catholic capitalist rather than for an unbelieving Socialist. In America the divisions in local elections are mainly on religious lines. This is no doubt convenient for the capitalists, and tends to make them religious men; but the capitalists alone could not produce the result. The result is produced by the fact that many working men prefer the advancement of their creed to the improvement of their livelihood. However deplorable such a state of mind may be, it is not necessarily due to capitalist lies.

All politics are governed by human desires. The materialist theory of history, in the last analysis, requires the assumption that every politically conscious person is governed by one single desire—the desire to increase his own share of commodities; and, further, that his method of achieving this desire will usually be to seek to increase the share of his class, not only his own individual share. But this assumption is very far from the truth. Men desire power, they desire satisfactions for their pride and their self-respect. They desire victory over rivals so profoundly that they will invent a rivalry for the unconscious purpose of making a victory possible. All these motives cut across the pure economic motive in ways that are practically important.

There is need of a treatment of political motives by the methods of psycho-analysis. In politics, as in private life, men invent myths to rationalize their conduct. If a man thinks that the only reasonable motive in politics is economic self-advancement, he will persuade himself that the things he wishes to do will make him rich. When he wants to fight the Germans, he tells himself that their competition is ruining his trade. If, on the other hand, he is an "idealist," who holds that his politics should aim at the advancement of the human race, he will tell himself that the crimes of the Germans demand their humiliation. The Marxian sees through this latter camouflage, but not through the former. To desire one's own economic advancement is comparatively reasonable; to Marx, who inherited eighteenth-century rationalist psychology from the British orthodox economists, self-enrichment seemed the natural aim of a man's political actions. But modern psychology has dived much deeper into the ocean of insanity upon which the little barque of human reason insecurely floats. The intellectual optimism of a bygone age is no longer possible to the modern student of human nature. Yet it lingers in Marxism, making Marxians rigid and Procrustean in their treatment of the life of instinct. Of this rigidity the materialistic conception of history is a prominent instance.

In the next chapter I shall attempt to outline a political psychology which seems to me more nearly true than that of Marx.

II ToC
DECIDING FORCES IN POLITICS

The larger events in the political life of the world are determined by the interaction of material conditions and human passions. The operation of the passions on the material conditions is modified by intelligence. The passions themselves may be modified by alien intelligence guided by alien passions. So far, such modification has been wholly unscientific, but it may in time become as precise as engineering.

The classification of the passions which is most convenient in political theory is somewhat different from that which would be adopted in psychology.

We may begin with desires for the necessaries of life: food, drink, sex, and (in cold climates) clothing and housing. When these are threatened, there is no limit to the activity and violence that men will display.

Planted upon these primitive desires are a number of secondary desires. Love of property, of which the fundamental political importance is obvious, may be derived historically and psychologically from the hoarding instinct. Love of the good opinion of others (which we may call vanity) is a desire which man shares with many animals; it is perhaps derivable from courtship, but has great survival value, among gregarious animals, in regard to others besides possible mates. Rivalry and love of power are perhaps developments of jealousy; they are akin, but not identical.

These four passions—acquisitiveness, vanity, rivalry, and love of power—are, after the basic instincts, the prime movers of almost all that happens in politics. Their operation is intensified and regularized by herd instinct. But herd instinct, by its very nature, cannot be a prime mover, since it merely causes the herd to act in unison, without determining what the united action is to be. Among men, as among other gregarious animals, the united action, in any given circumstances, is determined partly by the common passions of the herd, partly by imitation of leaders. The art of politics consists in causing the latter to prevail over the former.

Of the four passions we have enumerated, only one, namely acquisitiveness, is concerned at all directly with men's relations to their material conditions. The other three—vanity, rivalry, and love of power—are concerned with social relations. I think this is the source of what is erroneous in the Marxian interpretation of history, which tacitly assumes that acquisitiveness is the source of all political actions. It is clear that many men willingly forego wealth for the sake of power and glory, and that nations habitually sacrifice riches to rivalry with other nations. The desire for some form of superiority is common to almost all energetic men. No social system which attempts to thwart it can be stable, since the lazy majority will never be a match for the energetic minority.

What is called "virtue" is an offshoot of vanity: it is the habit of acting in a manner which others praise.

The operation of material conditions may be illustrated by the statement (Myers's *Dawn of History*) that four of the greatest movements of conquest have been due to drought in Arabia, causing the nomads of that country to migrate into regions already inhabited. The last of these four movements was the rise of Islam. In these four cases, the primal need of food and drink was enough to set events in motion; but as this need could only be satisfied by conquest, the four secondary passions must have very soon come into play. In the conquests of modern industrialism, the secondary passions have been almost wholly dominant, since those who directed them had no need to fear hunger or thirst. It is the potency of vanity and love of power that gives hope for the industrial future of Soviet Russia, since it enables the Communist State to enlist in its service men whose abilities might give them vast wealth in a capitalistic society.

Intelligence modifies profoundly the operation of material conditions. When America was first discovered, men only desired gold and silver; consequently the portions first settled were not those that are now most profitable. The Bessemer process created the German iron and steel industry; inventions requiring oil have created a demand for that commodity which is one of the chief influences in international politics.

The intelligence which has this profound effect on politics is not political, but scientific and technical: it is the kind of intelligence which discovers how to make nature minister to human passions. Tungsten had no value until it was found to be useful in the manufacture of shells and electric light, but now people will, if necessary, kill each other in order to acquire tungsten. Scientific intelligence is the cause of this change.

The progress or retrogression of the world depends, broadly speaking, upon the balance between acquisitiveness and rivalry. The former makes for progress, the latter for retrogression. When intelligence provides improved methods of production, these may be employed to increase the general share of goods, or to set apart more of the labour power of the community for the business of killing its rivals. Until 1914, acquisitiveness had prevailed, on the whole, since the fall of Napoleon; the past six years have seen a prevalence of the instinct of rivalry. Scientific intelligence makes it possible to indulge this instinct more fully than is possible for primitive peoples, since it sets free more men from the labour of producing necessaries. It is possible that scientific intelligence may, in time, reach the point when it will enable rivalry to exterminate the human race. This is the most hopeful method of bringing about an end of war.

For those who do not like this method, there is another: the study of scientific psychology and physiology. The physiological causes of emotions have begun to be known, through the studies of such men as Cannon (*Bodily Changes in Pain, Hunger, Fear and Rage*). In time, it may become possible, by physiological means, to alter the whole emotional nature of a population. It will then depend upon the passions of the rulers how this power is used. Success will come to the State which discovers how to promote pugnacity to the extent required for external war, but not to the extent which would lead to domestic dissensions. There is no method by which it can be insured that rulers shall desire the good of mankind, and therefore there is no reason to suppose that the power to modify men's emotional nature would cause progress.

If men desired to diminish rivalry, there is an obvious method. Habits of power intensify the passion of rivalry; therefore a State in which power is concentrated will, other things being equal, be more bellicose than one in which power is diffused. For those who dislike wars, this is an additional argument against all forms of dictatorship. But dislike of war is far less common than we used to suppose; and those who like war can use the same argument to support dictatorship.

III
BOLSHEVIK CRITICISM OF DEMOCRACY

The Bolshevik argument against Parliamentary democracy as a method of achieving Socialism is a powerful one. My answer to it lies rather in pointing out what I believe to be fallacies in the Bolshevik method, from which I conclude that no swift method exists of establishing any desirable form of Socialism. But let us first see what the Bolshevik argument is.

In the first place, it assumes that those to whom it is addressed are absolutely certain that Communism is desirable, so certain that they are willing, if necessary, to force it upon an unwilling population at the point of the bayonet. It then proceeds to argue that, while capitalism retains its hold over propaganda and its means of corruption, Parliamentary methods are very unlikely to give a majority for Communism in the House of Commons, or to lead to effective action by such a majority even if it existed. Communists point out how the people are deceived, and how their chosen leaders have again and again betrayed them. From this they argue that the destruction of capitalism must be sudden and catastrophic; that it must be the work of a minority; and that it cannot be effected constitutionally or without violence. It is therefore, in their view, the duty of the Communist party in a capitalist country to prepare for armed conflict, and to take all possible measure for disarming the bourgeoisie and arming that part of the proletariat which is willing to support the Communists.

There is an air of realism and disillusionment about this position, which makes it attractive to those idealists who wish to think themselves cynics. But I think there are various points in which it fails to be as realistic as it pretends.

In the first place, it makes much of the treachery of Labour leaders in constitutional movements, but does not consider the possibility of the treachery of Communist leaders in a revolution. To this the Marxian would reply that in constitutional movements men are bought, directly or indirectly, by the money of the capitalists, but that revolutionary Communism would leave the capitalists no money with which to attempt corruption. This has been achieved in Russia, and could be achieved elsewhere. But selling oneself to the capitalists is not the only possible form of treachery. It is also possible, having acquired power, to use it for one's own ends instead of for the people. This is what I believe to be likely to happen in Russia: the establishment of a bureaucratic aristocracy, concentrating authority in its own hands, and creating a régime just as oppressive and cruel as that of capitalism. Marxians never sufficiently recognize that love of power is quite as strong a motive, and quite as great a source of injustice, as love of money; yet this must be obvious to any unbiased student of politics. It is also obvious that the method of violent revolution leading to a minority dictatorship is one peculiarly calculated to create habits of despotism which would survive the crisis by which they were generated. Communist politicians are likely to become just like the politicians of other parties: a few will be honest, but the great majority will merely cultivate the art of telling a plausible tale with a view to tricking the people into entrusting them with power. The only possible way by which politicians as a class can be improved is the political and psychological education of the people, so that they may learn to detect a humbug. In England men have reached the point of suspecting a good speaker, but if a man speaks badly they think he must be honest. Unfortunately, virtue is not so widely diffused as this theory would imply.

In the second place, it is assumed by the Communist argument that, although capitalist propaganda can prevent the majority from becoming Communists, yet capitalist laws and police forces cannot prevent the Communists, while still a minority, from acquiring a supremacy of military power. It is thought that secret propaganda can undermine the army and navy, although it is admittedly impossible to get the majority to vote at elections for the programme of the Bolsheviks. This view is based upon Russian experience, where the army and navy had suffered defeat and had been brutally ill used by incompetent Tsarist authorities. The argument has no application to more efficient and successful States. Among the Germans, even in defeat, it was the civilian population that began the revolution.

There is a further assumption in the Bolshevik argument which seems to me quite unwarrantable. It is assumed that the capitalist governments will have learned nothing from the experience of Russia. Before the Russian Revolution, governments had not studied Bolshevik theory. And defeat in war created a revolutionary mood throughout Central and Eastern Europe. But now the holders of power are on their guard. There seems no reason whatever to suppose that they will supinely permit a preponderance of armed force to pass into the hands of those who wish to overthrow them, while, according to the Bolshevik theory, they are still sufficiently popular to be supported by a majority at the polls. Is it not as clear as noonday that in a democratic country it is more difficult for the proletariat to destroy the Government by arms than to defeat it in a general election? Seeing the immense advantages of a Government in dealing with rebels, it seems clear that rebellion could have little hope of success unless a very large majority supported it. Of course, if the army and navy were specially revolutionary, they might effect an unpopular revolution; but this situation, though something like it occurred in Russia, is hardly to be expected in the Western nations. This whole Bolshevik theory of revolution by a minority is one which might just conceivably have succeeded as a secret plot, but becomes impossible as soon as it is openly avowed and advocated.

But perhaps it will be said that I am caricaturing the Bolshevik doctrine of revolution. It is urged by advocates of this doctrine, quite truly, that all political events are brought about by minorities, since the majority are indifferent to politics. But there is a difference between a minority in which the indifferent acquiesce, and a minority so hated as to startle the indifferent into belated action. To make the Bolshevik doctrine reasonable, it is necessary to suppose that they believe the majority can be induced to acquiesce, at least temporarily, in the revolution made by the class-conscious minority. This, again, is based upon Russian experience: desire for peace and land led to a widespread support of the Bolsheviks in November 1917 on the part of people who have subsequently shown no love for Communism.

I think we come here to an essential part of Bolshevik philosophy. In the moment of revolution, Communists are to have some popular cry by which they win more support than mere Communism could win. Having thus acquired the State machine, they are to use it for their own ends. But this, again, is a method which can only be practised successfully so long as it is not avowed. It is to some extent habitual in politics. The Unionists in 1900 won a majority on the Boer War, and used it to endow brewers and Church schools. The Liberals in 1906 won a majority on Chinese labour, and used it to cement the secret alliance with France and to make an alliance with Tsarist Russia. President Wilson, in 1916, won his majority on neutrality, and used it to come into the war. This method is part of the stock-in-trade of democracy. But its success depends upon repudiating it until the moment comes to practise it. Those who, like the Bolsheviks, have the honesty to proclaim in advance their intention of using power for other ends than those for which it was given them, are not likely to have a chance of carrying out their designs.

What seems to me to emerge from these considerations is this: That in a democratic and politically educated country, armed revolution in favour of Communism would have no chance of succeeding unless it were supported by a larger majority than would be required for the election of a Communist Government by constitutional methods. It is possible that, if such a Government came into existence, and proceeded to carry out its programme, it would be met by armed resistance on the part of capital, including a large proportion of the officers in the army and navy. But in subduing this resistance it would have the support of that great body of opinion which believes in legality and upholds the constitution. Moreover, having, by hypothesis, converted a majority of the nation, a Communist Government could be sure of loyal help from immense numbers of workers, and would not be forced, as the Bolsheviks are in Russia, to suspect treachery everywhere. Under these circumstances, I believe that the resistance of the capitalists could be quelled without much difficulty, and would receive little support from moderate people. Whereas, in a minority revolt of Communists against a capitalist Government, all moderate opinion would be on the side of capitalism.

The contention that capitalist propaganda is what prevents the adoption of Communism by wage-earners is only very partially true. Capitalist propaganda has never been able to prevent the Irish from voting against the English, though it has been applied to this object with great vigour. It has proved itself powerless, over and over again, in opposing nationalist movements which had almost no moneyed support. It has been unable to cope with religious feeling. And those industrial populations which would most obviously benefit by Socialism have, in the main, adopted it, in spite of the opposition of employers. The plain truth is that Socialism does not arouse the same passionate interest in the average citizen as is roused by nationality and used to be roused by religion. It is not unlikely that things may change in this respect: we may be approaching a period of economic civil wars comparable to that of the religious civil wars that followed the Reformation. In such a period, nationalism is submerged by party: British and German Socialists, or British and German capitalists, will feel more kinship with each other than with compatriots of the opposite political camp. But when that day comes, there will be no difficulty, in highly industrial countries, in securing Socialist majorities; if Socialism is not then carried without bloodshed, it will be due to the unconstitutional action of the rich, not to the need of revolutionary violence on the part of the advocates of the proletariat. Whether such a state of opinion grows up or not depends mainly upon the stubbornness or conciliatoriness of the possessing classes, and, conversely, upon the moderation or violence of those who desire fundamental economic change. The majority which Bolsheviks regard as unattainable is chiefly prevented by the ruthlessness of their own tactics.

Apart from all arguments of detail, there are two broad objections to violent revolution in a democratic community. The first is that, when once the principle of respecting majorities as expressed at the ballot-box is abandoned, there is no reason to suppose that victory will be secured by the particular minority to which one happens to belong. There are many minorities besides Communists: religious minorities, teetotal minorities, militarist minorities, capitalist minorities. Any one of these could adopt the method of obtaining power advocated by the Bolsheviks, and any one would be just as likely to succeed as they are. What restrains these minorities, more or less, at present, is respect for the law and the constitution. Bolsheviks tacitly assume that every other party will preserve this respect while they themselves, unhindered, prepare the revolution. But if their philosophy of violence becomes popular, there is not the slightest reason to suppose that they will be its beneficiaries. They believe that Communism is for the good of the majority; they ought to believe that they can persuade the majority on this question, and to have the patience to set about the task of winning by propaganda.

The second argument of principle against the method of minority violence is that abandonment of law, when it becomes widespread, lets loose the wild beast, and gives a free rein to the primitive lusts and egoisms which civilization in some degree curbs. Every student of mediæval thought must have been struck by the extraordinarily high value placed upon law in that period. The reason was that, in countries infested by robber barons, law was the first requisite of progress. We, in the modern world, take it for granted that most people will be law-abiding, and we hardly realize what centuries of effort have gone to making such an assumption possible. We forget how many of the good things that we unquestionably expect would disappear out of life if murder, rape, and robbery with violence became common. And we forget even more how very easily this might happen. The universal class-war foreshadowed by the Third International, following upon the loosening of restraints produced by the late war, and combined with a deliberate inculcation of disrespect for law and constitutional government, might, and I believe would, produce a state of affairs in which it would be habitual to murder men for a crust of bread, and in which women would only be safe while armed men protected them. The civilized nations have accepted democratic government as a method of settling internal disputes without violence. Democratic government may have all the faults attributed to it, but it has the one great merit that people are, on the whole, willing to accept it as a substitute for civil war in political disputes. Whoever sets to work to weaken this acceptance, whether in Ulster or in Moscow, is taking a fearful responsibility. Civilization is not so stable that it cannot be broken up; and a condition of lawless violence is not one out of which any good thing is likely to emerge. For this reason, if for no other, revolutionary violence in a democracy is infinitely dangerous.

IV ToC
REVOLUTION AND DICTATORSHIP

The Bolsheviks have a very definite programme for achieving Communism—a programme which has been set forth by Lenin repeatedly, and quite recently in the reply of the Third International to the questionnaire submitted by the Independent Labour Party.

Capitalists, we are assured, will stick at nothing in defence of their privileges. It is the nature of man, in so far as he is politically conscious, to fight for the interests of his class so long as classes exist. When the conflict is not pushed to extremes, methods of conciliation and political deception may be preferable to actual physical warfare; but as soon as the proletariat make a really vital attack upon the capitalists, they will be met by guns and bayonets. This being certain and inevitable, it is as well to be prepared for it, and to conduct propaganda accordingly. Those who pretend that pacific methods can lead to the realization of Communism are false friends to the wage-earners; intentionally or unintentionally, they are covert allies of the bourgeoisie.

There must, then, according to Bolshevik theory, be armed conflict sooner or later, if the injustices of the present economic system are ever to be remedied. Not only do they assume armed conflict: they have a fairly definite conception of the way in which it is to be conducted. This conception has been carried out in Russia, and is to be carried out, before very long, in every civilized country. The Communists, who represent the class-conscious wage-earners, wait for some propitious moment when events have caused a mood of revolutionary discontent with the existing Government. They then put themselves at the head of the discontent, carry through a successful revolution, and in so doing acquire the arms, the railways, the State treasure, and all the other resources upon which the power of modern Governments is built. They then confine political power to Communists, however small a minority they may be of the whole nation. They set to work to increase their number by propaganda and the control of education. And meanwhile, they introduce Communism into every department of economic life as quickly as possible.

Ultimately, after a longer or shorter period, according to circumstances, the nation will be converted to Communism, the relics of capitalist institutions will have been obliterated, and it will be possible to restore freedom. But the political conflicts to which we are accustomed will not reappear. All the burning political questions of our time, according to the Communists, are questions of class conflict, and will disappear when the division of classes disappears. Accordingly the State will no longer be required, since the State is essentially an engine of power designed to give the victory to one side in the class conflict. Ordinary States are designed to give the victory to the capitalists; the proletarian State (Soviet Russia) is designed to give the victory to the wage-earners. As soon as the community contains only wage-earners, the State will cease to have any functions. And so, through a period of dictatorship, we shall finally arrive at a condition very similar to that aimed at by Anarchist Communism.

Three questions arise in regard to this method of reaching Utopia. First, would the ultimate state foreshadowed by the Bolsheviks be desirable in itself? Secondly, would the conflict involved in achieving it by the Bolshevik method be so bitter and prolonged that its evils would outweigh the ultimate good? Thirdly, is this method likely to lead, in the end, to the state which the Bolsheviks desire, or will it fail at some point and arrive at a quite different result? If we are to be Bolsheviks, we must answer all these questions in a sense favourable to their programme.

As regards the first question, I have no hesitation in answering it in a manner favourable to Communism. It is clear that the present inequalities of wealth are unjust. In part, they may be defended as affording an incentive to useful industry, but I do not think this defence will carry us very far. However, I have argued this question before in my book on *Roads to Freedom*, and I will not spend time upon it now. On this matter, I concede the Bolshevik case. It is the other two questions that I wish to discuss.

Our second question was: Is the ultimate good aimed at by the Bolsheviks sufficiently great to be worth the price that, according to their own theory, will have to be paid for achieving it?

If anything human were absolutely certain, we might answer this question affirmatively with some confidence. The benefits of Communism, if it were once achieved, might be expected to be lasting; we might legitimately hope that further change would be towards something still better, not towards a revival of ancient evils. But if we admit, as we must do, that the outcome of the Communist revolution is in some degree uncertain, it becomes necessary to count the cost; for a great part of the cost is all but certain.

Since the revolution of October, 1917, the Soviet Government has been at war with almost all the world, and has had at the same time to face civil war at home. This is not to be regarded as accidental, or as a misfortune which could not be foreseen. According to Marxian theory, what has happened was bound to happen. Indeed, Russia has been wonderfully fortunate in not having to face an even more desperate situation. First and foremost, the world was exhausted by the war, and in no mood for military adventures. Next, the Tsarist régime was the worst in Europe, and therefore rallied less support than would be secured by any other capitalist Government. Again, Russia is vast and agricultural, making it capable of resisting both invasion and blockade better than Great Britain or France or Germany. The only other country that could have resisted with equal success is the United States, which is at present very far removed from a proletarian revolution, and likely long to remain the chief bulwark of the capitalist system. It is evident that Great Britain, attempting a similar revolution, would be forced by starvation to yield within a few months, provided America led a policy of blockade. The same is true, though in a less degree, of continental countries. Therefore, unless and until an international Communist revolution becomes possible, we must expect that any other nation following Russia's example will have to pay an even higher price than Russia has had to pay.

Now the price that Russia is having to pay is very great. The almost universal poverty might be thought to be a small evil in comparison with the ultimate gain, but it brings with it other evils of which the magnitude would be acknowledged even by those who have never known poverty and therefore make light of it. Hunger brings an absorption in the question of food, which, to most people, makes life almost purely animal. The general shortage makes people fierce, and reacts upon the political atmosphere. The necessity of inculcating Communism produces a hot-house condition, where every breath of fresh air must be excluded: people are to be taught to think in a certain way, and all free intelligence becomes taboo. The country comes to resemble an immensely magnified Jesuit College. Every kind of liberty is banned as being "*bourgeois*"; but it remains a fact that intelligence languishes where thought is not free.

All this, however, according to the leaders of the Third International, is only a small beginning of the struggle, which must become world-wide before it achieves victory. In their reply to the Independent Labour Party they say:

It is probable that upon the throwing off of the chains of the capitalist Governments, the revolutionary proletariat of Europe will meet the resistance of Anglo-Saxon capital in the persons of British and American capitalists who will attempt to blockade it. It is then possible that the revolutionary proletariat of Europe will rise in union with the peoples of the East and commence a revolutionary struggle, the scene of which will be the entire world, to deal a final blow to British and American capitalism (*The Times*, July 30, 1920).

The war here prophesied, if it ever takes place, will be one compared to which the late war will come to seem a mere affair of outposts. Those who realize the destructiveness of the late war, the devastation and impoverishment, the lowering of the level of civilization throughout vast areas, the general increase of hatred and savagery, the letting loose of bestial instincts which had been curbed during peace—those who realize all this will hesitate to incur inconceivably greater horrors, even if they believe firmly that Communism in itself is much to be desired. An economic system cannot be considered apart from the population which is to carry it out; and the population resulting from such a world-war as Moscow calmly contemplates would be savage, bloodthirsty and ruthless to an extent that must make any system a mere engine of oppression and cruelty.

This brings us to our third question: Is the system which Communists regard as their goal likely to result from the adoption of their methods? This is really the most vital question of the three.

Advocacy of Communism by those who believe in Bolshevik methods rests upon the assumption that there is no slavery except economic slavery, and that when all goods are held in common there must be perfect liberty. I fear this is a delusion.

There must be administration, there must be officials who control distribution. These men, in a Communist State, are the repositories of power. So long as they control the army, they are able, as in Russia at this moment, to wield despotic power even if they are a small minority. The fact that there is Communism—to a certain extent—does not mean that there is liberty. If the Communism were more complete, it would not necessarily mean more freedom; there would still be certain officials in control of the food supply, and these officials could govern as they pleased so long as they retained the support of the soldiers. This is not mere theory: it is the patent lesson of the present condition of Russia. The Bolshevik theory is that a small minority are to seize power, and are to hold it until Communism is accepted practically universally, which, they admit, may take a long time. But power is sweet, and few men surrender it voluntarily. It is especially sweet to those who have the habit of it, and the habit becomes most ingrained in those who have governed by bayonets, without popular support. Is it not almost inevitable that men placed as the Bolsheviks are placed in Russia, and as they maintain that the Communists must place themselves wherever the social revolution succeeds, will be loath to relinquish their monopoly of power, and will find reasons for remaining until some new revolution ousts them? Would it not be fatally easy for them, without altering economic structure, to decree large salaries for high Government officials, and so reintroduce the old inequalities of wealth? What motive would they have for not doing so? What motive is possible except idealism, love of mankind, non-economic motives of the sort that Bolsheviks decry? The system created by violence and the forcible rule of a minority must necessarily allow of tyranny and exploitation; and if human nature is what Marxians assert it to be, why should the rulers neglect such opportunities of selfish advantage?

It is sheer nonsense to pretend that the rulers of a great empire such as Soviet Russia, when they have become accustomed to power, retain the proletarian psychology, and feel that their class-interest is the same as that of the ordinary working man. This is not the case in fact in Russia now, however the truth may be concealed by fine phrases. The Government has a class-consciousness and a class-interest quite distinct from those of the genuine proletarian, who is not to be confounded with the paper proletarian of the Marxian schema. In a capitalist state, the Government and the capitalists on the whole hang together, and form one class; in Soviet Russia, the Government has absorbed the capitalist mentality together with the governmental, and the fusion has given increased strength to the upper class. But I see no reason whatever to expect equality or freedom to result from such a system, except reasons derived from a false psychology and a mistaken analysis of the sources of political power.

I am compelled to reject Bolshevism for two reasons: First, because the price mankind must pay to achieve Communism by Bolshevik methods is too terrible; and secondly because, even after paying the price, I do not believe the result would be what the Bolsheviks profess to desire.

But if their methods are rejected, how are we ever to arrive at a better economic system? This is not an easy question, and I shall treat it in a separate chapter.

V ToC
MECHANISM AND THE INDIVIDUAL

Is it possible to effect a fundamental reform of the existing economic system by any other method than that of Bolshevism? The difficulty of answering this question is what chiefly attracts idealists to the dictatorship of the proletariat. If, as I have argued, the method of violent revolution and Communist rule is not likely to have the results which idealists desire, we are reduced to despair unless we can see hope in other methods. The Bolshevik arguments against all other methods are powerful. I confess that, when the spectacle of present-day Russia forced me to disbelieve in Bolshevik methods, I was at first unable to see any way of curing the essential evils of capitalism. My first impulse was to abandon political thinking as a bad job, and to conclude that the strong and ruthless must always exploit the weaker and kindlier sections of the population. But this is not an attitude that can be long maintained by any vigorous and temperamentally hopeful person. Of course, if it were the truth, one would have to acquiesce. Some people believe that by living on sour milk one can achieve immortality. Such optimists are answered by a mere refutation; it is not necessary to go on and point out some other way of escaping death. Similarly an argument that Bolshevism will not lead to the millennium would remain valid even if it could be shown that the millennium cannot be reached by any other road. But the truth in social questions is not quite like truth in physiology or physics, since it depends upon men's beliefs. Optimism tends to verify itself by making people impatient of avoidable evils; while despair, on the other hand, makes the world as bad as it believes it to be. It is therefore imperative for those who do not believe in Bolshevism to put some other hope in its place.

I think there are two things that must be admitted: first, that many of the worst evils of capitalism might survive under Communism; secondly, that the cure for these evils cannot be sudden, since it requires changes in the average mentality.

What are the chief evils of the present system? I do not think that mere inequality of wealth, in itself, is a very grave evil. If everybody had enough, the fact that some have more than enough would be unimportant. With a very moderate improvement in methods of production, it would be easy to ensure that everybody should have enough, even under capitalism, if wars and preparations for wars were abolished. The problem of poverty is by no means insoluble within the existing system, except when account is taken of psychological factors and the uneven distribution of power.

The graver evils of the capitalist system all arise from its uneven distribution of power. The possessors of capital wield an influence quite out of proportion to their numbers or their services to the community. They control almost the whole of education and the press; they decide what the average man shall know or not know; the cinema has given them a new method of propaganda, by which they enlist the support of those who are too frivolous even for illustrated papers. Very little of the intelligence of the world is really free: most of it is, directly or indirectly, in the pay of business enterprises or wealthy philanthropists. To satisfy capitalist interests, men are compelled to work much harder and more monotonously than they ought to work, and their education is scamped. Wherever, as in barbarous or semi-civilized countries, labour is too weak or too disorganized to protect itself, appalling cruelties are practised for private profit. Economic and political organizations become more and more vast, leaving less and less room for individual development and initiative. It is this sacrifice of the individual to the machine that is the fundamental evil of the modern world.

To cure this evil is not easy, because efficiency is promoted, at any given moment, though not in the long run, by sacrificing the individual to the smooth working of a vast organization, whether military or industrial. In war and in commercial competition, it is necessary to control individual impulses, to treat men as so many "bayonets" or "sabres" or "hands," not as a society of separate people with separate tastes and capacities. Some sacrifice of individual impulses is, of course, essential to the existence of an ordered community, and this degree of sacrifice is, as a rule, not regretable even from the individual's point of view. But what is demanded in a highly militarized or industrialized nation goes far beyond this very moderate degree. A society which is to allow much freedom to the individual must be strong enough to be not anxious about home defence, moderate enough to refrain from difficult external conquests, and rich enough to value leisure and a civilized existence more than an increase of consumable commodities.

But where the material conditions for such a state of affairs exist, the psychological conditions are not likely to exist unless power is very widely diffused throughout the community. Where power is concentrated in a few, it will happen, unless those few are very exceptional people, that they will value tangible achievements in the way of increase in trade or empire more than the slow and less obvious improvements that would result from better education combined with more leisure. The joys of victory are especially great to the holders of power, while the evils of a mechanical organization fall almost exclusively upon the less influential. For these reasons, I do not believe that any community in which power is much concentrated will long refrain from conflicts of the kind involving a sacrifice of what is most valuable in the individual. In Russia at this moment, the sacrifice of the individual is largely inevitable, because of the severity of the economic and military struggle. But I did not feel, in the Bolsheviks, any consciousness of the magnitude of this misfortune, or any realization of the importance of the individual as against the State. Nor do I believe that men who do realize this are likely to succeed, or to come to the top, in times when everything has to be done against personal liberty. The Bolshevik theory requires that every country, sooner or later, should go through what Russia is going through now. And in every country in such a condition we may expect to find the government falling into the hands of ruthless men, who have not by nature any love for freedom, and who will see little importance in hastening the transition from dictatorship to freedom. It is far more likely that such men will be tempted to embark upon new enterprises, requiring further concentration of forces, and postponing indefinitely the liberation of the populations which they use as their material.

For these reasons, equalization of wealth without equalization of power seems to me a rather small and unstable achievement. But equalization of power is not a thing that can be achieved in a day. It requires a considerable level of moral, intellectual, and technical education. It requires a long period without extreme crises, in order that habits of tolerance and good nature may become common. It requires vigour on the part of those who are acquiring power, without a too desperate resistance on the part of those whose share is diminishing. This is only possible if those who are acquiring power are not very fierce, and do not terrify their opponents by threats of ruin and death. It cannot be done quickly, because quick methods require that very mechanism and subordination of the individual which we should struggle to prevent.

But even equalization of power is not the whole of what is needed politically. The right grouping of men for different purposes is also essential. Self-government in industry, for example, is an indispensable condition of a good society. Those acts of an individual or a group which have no very great importance for outsiders ought to be freely decided by that individual or group. This is recognized as regards religion, but ought to be recognized over a much wider field.

Bolshevik theory seems to me to err by concentrating its attention upon one evil, namely inequality of wealth, which it believes to be at the bottom of all others. I do not believe any one evil can be thus isolated, but if I had to select one as the greatest of political evils, I should select inequality of power. And I should deny that this is likely to be cured by the class-war and the dictatorship of the Communist party. Only peace and a long period of gradual improvement can bring it about.

Good relations between individuals, freedom from hatred and violence and oppression, general diffusion of education, leisure rationally employed, the progress of art and science—these seem to me among the most important ends that a political theory ought to have in view. I do not believe that they can be furthered, except very rarely, by revolution and war; and I am convinced that at the present moment they can only be promoted by a diminution in the spirit of ruthlessness generated by the war. For these reasons, while admitting the necessity and even utility of Bolshevism in Russia, I do not wish to see it spread, or to encourage the adoption of its philosophy by advanced parties in the Western nations.

VIToC
WHY RUSSIAN COMMUNISM HAS FAILED

The civilized world seems almost certain, sooner or later, to follow the example of Russia in attempting a Communist organization of society. I believe that the attempt is essential to the progress and happiness of mankind during the next few centuries, but I believe also that the transition has appalling dangers. I believe that, if the Bolshevik theory as to the method of transition is adopted by Communists in Western nations, the result will be a prolonged chaos, leading neither to Communism nor to any other civilized system, but to a relapse into the barbarism of the Dark Ages. In the interests of Communism, no less than in the interests of civilization, I think it imperative that the Russian failure should be admitted and analysed. For this reason, if for no other, I cannot enter into the conspiracy of concealment which many Western Socialists who have visited Russia consider necessary.

I shall try first to recapitulate the facts which make me regard the Russian experiment as a failure, and then to seek out the causes of failure.

The most elementary failure in Russia is in regard to food. In a country which formerly produced a vast exportable surplus of cereals and other agricultural produce, and in which the non-agricultural population is only 15 per cent. of the total, it ought to be possible, without great difficulty, to provide enough food for the towns. Yet the Government has failed badly in this respect. The rations are inadequate and irregular, so that it is impossible to preserve health and vigour without the help of food purchased illicitly in the markets at speculative prices. I have given reasons for thinking that the breakdown of transport, though a contributory cause, is not the main reason for the shortage. The main reason is the hostility of the peasants, which, in turn, is due to the collapse of industry and to the policy of forced requisitions. In regard to corn and flour, the Government requisitions all that the peasant produces above a certain minimum required for himself and his family. If, instead, it exacted a fixed amount as rent, it would not destroy his incentive to production, and would not provide nearly such a strong motive for concealment. But this plan would have enabled the peasants to grow rich, and would have involved a confessed abandonment of Communist theory. It has therefore been thought better to employ forcible methods, which led to disaster, as they were bound to do.

The collapse of industry was the chief cause of the food difficulties, and has in turn been aggravated by them. Owing to the fact that there is abundant food in the country, industrial and urban workers are perpetually attempting to abandon their employment for agriculture. This is illegal, and is severely punished, by imprisonment or convict labour. Nevertheless it continues, and in so vast a country as Russia it is not possible to prevent it. Thus the ranks of industry become still further depleted.

Except as regards munitions of war, the collapse of industry in Russia is extraordinarily complete. The resolutions passed by the Ninth Congress of the Communist Party (April, 1920) speak of "the incredible catastrophes of public economy." This language is not too strong, though the recovery of the Baku oil has done something to produce a revival along the Volga basin.

The failure of the whole industrial side of the national economy, including transport, is at the bottom of the other failures of the Soviet Government. It is, to begin with, the main cause of the unpopularity of the Communists both in town and country: in town, because the people are hungry; in the country, because food is taken with no return except paper. If industry had been prosperous, the peasants could have had clothes and agricultural machinery, for which they would have willingly parted with enough food for the needs of the towns. The town population could then have subsisted in tolerable comfort; disease could have been coped with, and the general lowering of vitality averted. It would not have been necessary, as it has been in many cases, for men of scientific or artistic capacity to abandon the pursuits in which they were skilled for unskilled manual labour. The Communist Republic might have been agreeable to live in—at least for those who had been very poor before.

The unpopularity of the Bolsheviks, which is primarily due to the collapse of industry, has in turn been accentuated by the measures which it has driven the Government to adopt. In view of the fact that it was impossible to give adequate food to the ordinary population of Petrograd and Moscow, the Government decided that at any rate the men employed on important public work should be sufficiently nourished to preserve their efficiency. It is a gross libel to say that the Communists, or even the leading People's Commissaries, live luxurious lives according to our standards; but it is a fact that they are not exposed, like their subjects, to acute hunger and the weakening of energy that accompanies it. No tone can blame them for this, since the work of government must be carried on; but it is one of the ways in which class distinctions have reappeared where it was intended that they should be banished. I talked to an obviously hungry working man in Moscow, who pointed to the Kremlin and remarked: "In there they have enough to eat." He was expressing a widespread feeling which is fatal to the idealistic appeal that Communism attempts to make.

Owing to unpopularity, the Bolsheviks have had to rely upon the army and the Extraordinary Commission, and have been compelled to reduce the Soviet system to an empty form. More and more the pretence of representing the proletariat has grown threadbare. Amid official demonstrations and processions and meetings the genuine proletarian looks on, apathetic and disillusioned, unless he is possessed of unusual energy and fire, in which case he looks to the ideas of syndicalism or the I.W.W. to liberate him from a slavery far more complete than that of capitalism. A sweated wage, long hours, industrial conscription, prohibition of strikes, prison for slackers, diminution of the already insufficient rations in factories where the production falls below what the authorities expect, an army of spies ready to report any tendency to political disaffection and to procure imprisonment for its promoters—this is the reality of a system which still professes to govern in the name of the proletariat.

At the same time the internal and external peril has necessitated the creation of a vast army recruited by conscription, except as regards a Communist nucleus, from among a population utterly weary of war, who put the Bolsheviks in power because they alone promised peace. Militarism has produced its inevitable result in the way of a harsh and dictatorial spirit: the men in power go through their day's work with the consciousness that they command three million armed men, and that civilian opposition to their will can be easily crushed.

Out of all this has grown a system painfully like the old government of the Tsar—a system which is Asiatic in its centralized bureaucracy, its secret service, its atmosphere of governmental mystery and submissive terror. In many ways it resembles our Government of India. Like that Government, it stands for civilization, for education, sanitation, and Western ideas of progress; it is composed in the main of honest and hard-working men, who despise those whom they govern, but believe themselves possessed of something valuable which they must communicate to the population, however little it may be desired. Like our Government in India, they live in terror of popular risings, and are compelled to resort to cruel repressions in order to preserve their power. Like it, they represent an alien philosophy of life, which cannot be forced upon the people without a change of instinct, habit, and tradition so profound as to dry up the vital springs of action, producing listlessness and despair among the ignorant victims of militant enlightenment. It may be that Russia needs sternness and discipline more than anything else; it may be that a revival of Peter the Great's methods is essential to progress. From this point of view, much of what it is natural to criticize in the Bolsheviks becomes defensible; but this point of view has little affinity to Communism. Bolshevism may be defended, possibly, as a dire discipline through which a backward nation is to be rapidly industrialized; but as an experiment in Communism it has failed.

There are two things that a defender of the Bolsheviks may say against the argument that they have failed because the present state of Russia is bad. It may be said that it is too soon to judge, and it may be urged that whatever failure there has been is attributable to the hostility of the outside world.

As to the contention that it is too soon to judge, that is of course undeniable in a sense. But in a sense it is always too soon to judge of any historical movement, because its effects and developments go on for ever. Bolshevism has, no doubt, great changes ahead of it. But the last three years have afforded material for some judgments, though more definitive judgments will be possible later. And, for reasons which I have given in earlier chapters, I find it impossible to believe that later developments will realize more fully the Communist ideal. If trade is opened with the outer world, there will be an almost irresistible tendency to resumption of private enterprise. If trade is not re-opened, the plans of Asiatic conquest will mature, leading to a revival of Yenghis Khan and Timur. In neither case is the purity of the Communist faith likely to survive.

As for the hostility of the Entente, it is of course true that Bolshevism might have developed very differently if it had been treated in a friendly spirit. But in view of its desire to promote world-revolution, no one could expect—and the Bolsheviks certainly did not expect—that capitalist Governments would be friendly. If Germany had won the war, Germany would have shown a hostility more effective than that of the Entente. However we may blame Western Governments for their policy, we must realize that, according to the deterministic economic theory of the Bolsheviks, no other policy was to be expected from them. Other men might have been excused for not foreseeing the attitude of Churchill, Clemenceau and Millerand; but Marxians could not be excused, since this attitude was in exact accord with their own formula.

We have seen the symptoms of Bolshevik failure; I come now to the question of its profounder causes.

Everything that is worst in Russia we found traceable to the collapse of industry. Why has industry collapsed so utterly? And would it collapse equally if a Communist revolution were to occur in a Western country?

Russian industry was never highly developed, and depended always upon outside aid for much of its plant. The hostility of the world, as embodied in the blockade, left Russia powerless to replace the machinery and locomotives worn out during the war. The need of self-defence compelled the Bolsheviks to send their best workmen to the front, because they were the most reliable Communists, and the loss of them rendered their factories even more inefficient than they were under Kerensky. In this respect, and in the laziness and incapacity of the Russian workman, the Bolsheviks have had to face special difficulties which would be less in other countries. On the other hand, they have had special advantages in the fact that Russia is self-supporting in the matter of food; no other country could have endured the collapse of industry so long, and no other Great Power except the United States could have survived years of blockade.

The hostility of the world was in no way a surprise to those who made the October revolution; it was in accordance with their general theory, and its consequences should have been taken into account in making the revolution.

Other hostilities besides those of the outside world have been incurred by the Bolsheviks with open eyes, notably the hostility of the peasants and that of a great part of the industrial population. They have attempted, in accordance with their usual contempt for conciliatory methods, to substitute terror for reward as the incentive to work. Some amiable Socialists have imagined that, when the private capitalist had been eliminated, men would work from a sense of obligation to the community. The Bolsheviks will have none of such sentimentalism. In one of the resolutions of the ninth Communist Congress they say:

Every social system, whether based on slavery, feudalism, or capitalism, had its ways and means of labour compulsion and labour education in the interests of the exploiters.

The Soviet system is faced with the task of developing its own methods of labour compulsion to attain an increase of the intensity and wholesomeness of labour; this method is to be based on the socialization of public economy in the interests of the whole nation.

In addition to the propaganda by which the people are to be influenced and the repressions which are to be applied to all idlers, parasites and disorganizers who strive to undermine public zeal—the principal method for the increase of production will become the introduction of the system of compulsory labour.

In capitalist society rivalry assumed the character of competition and led to the exploitation of man by man. In a society where the means of production are nationalized, labour rivalry is to increase the products of labour without infringing its solidarity.

Rivalry between factories, regions, guilds, workshops, and individual workers should become the subject of careful organization and of close study on the side of the Trade Unions and the economic organs.

The system of premiums which is to be introduced should become one of the most powerful means of exciting rivalry. The system of rationing of food supply is to get into line with it; so long as Soviet Russia suffers from insufficiency of provisions, it is only just that the industrious and conscientious worker receives more than the careless worker.

It must be remembered that even the "industrious and conscientious worker" receives less food than is required to maintain efficiency.

Over the whole development of Russia and of Bolshevism since the October revolution there broods a tragic fatality. In spite of outward success the inner failure has proceeded by inevitable stages—stages which could, by sufficient acumen, have been foreseen from the first. By provoking the hostility of the outside world the Bolsheviks were forced to provoke the hostility of the peasants, and finally the hostility or utter apathy of the urban and industrial population. These various hostilities brought material disaster, and material disaster brought spiritual collapse. The ultimate source of the whole train of evils lies in the Bolshevik outlook on life: in its dogmatism of hatred and its belief that human nature can be completely transformed by force. To injure capitalists is not the ultimate goal of Communism, though among men dominated by hatred it is the part that gives zest to their activities. To face the hostility of the world may show heroism, but it is a heroism for which the country, not its rulers, has to pay the price. In the principles of Bolshevism there is more desire to destroy ancient evils than to build up new goods; it is for this reason that success in destruction has been so much greater than in construction. The desire to destroy is inspired by hatred, which is not a constructive principle. From this essential characteristic of Bolshevik mentality has sprung the willingness to subject Russia to its present martyrdom. It is only out of a quite different mentality that a happier world can be created.

And from this follows a further conclusion. The Bolshevik outlook is the outcome of the cruelty of the Tsarist régime and the ferocity of the years of the Great War, operating upon a ruined and starving nation maddened into universal hatred. If a different mentality is needed for the establishment of a successful Communism, then a quite different conjuncture must see its inauguration; men must be persuaded to the attempt by hope, not driven to it by despair. To bring this about should be the aim of every Communist who desires the happiness of mankind more than the punishment of capitalists and their governmental satellites.

VII
CONDITIONS FOR THE SUCCESS OF COMMUNISM

The fundamental ideas of Communism are by no means impracticable, and would, if realized, add immeasurably to the well-being of mankind. The difficulties which have to be faced are not in regard to the fundamental ideas, but in regard to the transition from capitalism. It must be assumed that those who profit by the existing system will fight to preserve it, and their fight may be sufficiently severe to destroy all that is best in Communism during the struggle, as well as everything else that has value in modern civilization. The seriousness of this problem of transition is illustrated by Russia, and cannot be met by the methods of the Third International. The Soviet Government, at the present moment, is anxious to obtain manufactured goods from capitalist countries, but the Third International is meanwhile endeavouring to promote revolutions which, if they occurred, would paralyse the industries of the countries concerned, and leave them incapable of supplying Russian needs.

The supreme condition of success in a Communist revolution is that it should not paralyse industry. If industry is paralysed, the evils which exist in modern Russia, or others just as great, seem practically unavoidable. There will be the problem of town and country, there will be hunger, there will be fierceness and revolts and military tyranny. All these things follow in a fatal sequence; and the end of them is almost certain to be something quite different from what genuine Communists desire.

If industry is to survive throughout a Communist revolution, a number of conditions must be fulfilled which are not, at present, fulfilled anywhere. Consider, for the sake of definiteness, what would happen if a Communist revolution were to occur in England to-morrow. Immediately America would place an embargo on all trade with us. The cotton industry would collapse, leaving about five million of the most productive portion of the population idle. The food supply would become inadequate, and would fail disastrously if, as is to be expected, the Navy were hostile or disorganized by the sabotage of the officers. The result would be that, unless there were a counter-revolution, about half the population would die within the first twelve months. On such a basis it would evidently be impossible to erect a successful Communist State.

What applies to England applies, in one form or another, to the remaining countries of Europe. Italian and German Socialists are, many of them, in a revolutionary frame of mind and could, if they chose, raise formidable revolts. They are urged by Moscow to do so, but they realize that, if they did, England and America would starve them. France, for many reasons, dare not offend England and America beyond a point. Thus, in every country except America, a successful Communist revolution is impossible for economico-political reasons. America, being self-contained and strong, would be capable, so far as material conditions go, of achieving a successful revolution; but in America the psychological conditions are as yet adverse. There is no other civilized country where capitalism is so strong and revolutionary Socialism so weak as in America. At the present moment, therefore, though it is by no means impossible that Communist revolutions may occur all over the Continent, it is nearly certain that they cannot be successful in any real sense. They will have to begin by a war against America, and possibly England, by a paralysis of industry, by starvation, militarism and the whole attendant train of evils with which Russia has made us familiar.

That Communism, whenever and wherever it is adopted, will have to begin by fighting the bourgeoisie, is highly probable. The important question is not whether there is to be fighting, but how long and severe it is to be. A short war, in which Communism won a rapid and easy victory, would do little harm. It is long, bitter and doubtful wars that must be avoided if anything of what makes Communism desirable is to survive.

Two practical consequences flow from this conclusion: first, that nothing can succeed until America is either converted to Communism, or at any rate willing to remain neutral; secondly, that it is a mistake to attempt to inaugurate Communism in a country where the majority are hostile, or rather, where the active opponents are as strong as the active supporters, because in such a state of opinion a very severe civil war is likely to result. It is necessary to have a great body of opinion favourable to Communism, and a rather weak opposition, before a really successful Communist state can be introduced either by revolution or by more or less constitutional methods.

It may be assumed that when Communism is first introduced, the higher technical and business staff will side with the capitalists and attempt sabotage unless they have no hopes of a counter-revolution. For this reason it is very necessary that among wage-earners there should be as wide a diffusion as possible of technical and business education, so that they may be able immediately to take control of big complex industries. In this respect Russia was very badly off, whereas England and America would be much more fortunate.

Self-government in industry is, I believe, the road by which England can best approach Communism. I do not doubt that the railways and the mines, after a little practice, could be run more efficiently by the workers, from the point of view of production, than they are at present by the capitalists. The Bolsheviks oppose self-government in industry every where, because it has failed in Russia, and their national self-esteem prevents them from admitting that this is due to the backwardness of Russia. This is one of the respects in which they are misled by the assumption that Russia must be in all ways a model to the rest of the world. I would go so far as to say that the winning of self-government in such industries as railways and mining is an essential preliminary to complete Communism. In England, especially, this is the case. The Unions can command whatever technical skill they may require; they are politically powerful; the demand for self-government is one for which there is widespread sympathy, and could be much more with adequate propaganda; moreover (what is important with the British temperament) self-government can be brought about gradually, by stages in each trade, and by extension from one trade to another. Capitalists value two things, their power and their money; many individuals among them value only the money. It is wiser to concentrate first on the power, as is done by seeking self-government in industry without confiscation of capitalist incomes. By this means the capitalists are gradually turned into obvious drones, their active functions in industry become nil, and they can be ultimately dispossessed without dislocation and without the possibility of any successful struggle on their parts.

Another advantage of proceeding by way of self-government is that it tends to prevent the Communist régime, when it comes, from having that truly terrible degree of centralization which now exists in Russia. The Russians have been forced to centralize, partly by the problems of the war, but more by the shortage of all kinds of skill. This has compelled the few competent men to attempt each to do the work of ten men, which has not proved satisfactory in spite of heroic efforts. The idea of democracy has become discredited as the result first of syndicalism, and then of Bolshevism. But there are two different things that may be meant by democracy: we may mean the system of Parliamentary government, or we may mean the participation of the people in affairs. The discredit of the former is largely deserved, and I have no desire to uphold Parliament as an ideal institution. But it is a great misfortune if, from a confusion of ideas, men come to think that, because Parliaments are imperfect, there is no reason why there should be self-government. The grounds for advocating self-government are very familiar: first, that no benevolent despot can be trusted to know or pursue the interests of his subjects; second, that the practice of self-government is the only effective method of political education; third, that it tends to place the preponderance of force on the side of the constitution, and thus to promote order and stable government. Other reasons could be found, but I think these are the chief. In Russia self-government has disappeared, except within the Communist Party. If it is not to disappear elsewhere during a Communist revolution, it is very desirable that there should exist already important industries competently administered by the workers themselves.

The Bolshevik philosophy is promoted very largely by despair of more gradual methods. But this despair is a mark of impatience, and is not really warranted by the facts. It is by no means impossible, in the near future, to secure self-government in British railways and mines by constitutional means. This is not the sort of measure which would bring into operation an American blockade or a civil war or any of the other catastrophic dangers that are to be feared from a full-fledged Communist revolution in the present international situation. Self-government in industry is feasible, and would be a great step towards Communism. It would both afford many of the advantages of Communism and also make the transition far easier without a technical break-down of production.

There is another defect in the methods advocated by the Third International. The sort of revolution which is recommended is never practically feasible except in a time of national misfortune; in fact, defeat in war seems to be an indispensable condition. Consequently, by this method, Communism will only be inaugurated where the conditions of life are difficult, where demoralization and disorganization make success almost impossible, and where men are in a mood of fierce despair very inimical to industrial construction. If Communism is to have a fair chance, it must be inaugurated in a prosperous country. But a prosperous country will not be readily moved by the arguments of hatred and universal upheaval which are employed by the Third International. It is necessary, in appealing to a prosperous country, to lay stress on hope rather than despair, and to show how the transition can be effected without a calamitous loss of prosperity. All this requires less violence and subversiveness, more patience and constructive propaganda, less appeal to the armed might of a determined minority.

The attitude of uncompromising heroism is attractive, and appeals especially to the dramatic instinct. But the purpose of the serious revolutionary is not personal heroism, nor martyrdom, but the creation of a happier world. Those who have the happiness of the world at heart will shrink from attitudes and the facile hysteria of "no parley with the enemy." They will not embark upon enterprises, however arduous and austere, which are likely to involve the martyrdom of their country and the discrediting of their ideals. It is by slower and less showy methods that the new world must be built: by industrial efforts after self-government, by proletarian training in technique and business administration, by careful study of the international situation, by a prolonged and devoted propaganda of ideas rather than tactics, especially among the wage-earners of the United States. It is not true that no gradual approaches to Communism are possible: self-government in industry is an important instance to the contrary. It is not true that any isolated European country, or even the whole of the Continent in unison, can, after the exhaustion produced by the war, introduce a successful form of Communism at the present moment, owing to the hostility and economic supremacy of America. To find fault with those who urge these considerations, or to accuse them of faint-heartedness, is mere sentimental self-indulgence, sacrificing the good we can do to the satisfaction of our own emotions.

Even under present conditions in Russia, it is possible still to feel the inspiration of the essential spirit of Communism, the spirit of creative hope, seeking to sweep away the incumbrances of injustice and tyranny and rapacity which obstruct the growth of the human spirit, to replace individual competition by collective action, the relation of master and slave by free co-operation. This hope has helped the best of the Communists to bear the harsh years through which Russia has been passing, and has become an inspiration to the world. The hope is not chimerical, but it can only be realized through a more patient labour, a more objective study of facts, and above all a longer propaganda, to make the necessity of the transition obvious to the great majority of wage-earners. Russian Communism may fail and go under, but Communism itself will not die. And if hope rather than hatred inspires its advocates, it can be brought about without the universal cataclysm preached by Moscow. The war and its sequel have proved the destructiveness of capitalism; let us see to it that the next epoch does not prove the still greater destructiveness of Communism, but rather its power to heal the wounds which the old evil system has inflicted upon the human spirit.

Milton Keynes UK
Ingram Content Group UK Ltd.
UKHW050241220624
444555UK00005BA/468